Advance Praise for

Un-Surprise Me!

"Get ready to be surprised by *Un-Surprise Me!* The first book on finances, of many I have read, that puts Life Planning as the horse and Financial Planning as the cart. Candid, clear, concise, and comprehensive, *Un-Surprise Me!* thoughtfully demystifies the world of financial planning through a refreshing lens. This book has all the hallmarks of successful strategic planning—practicality, pragmatism, and executability!"

— CHRISTOPHER P. MCPADDEN
Major General (R), US Army

"Wheeler's *Un-Surprise Me!* masterfully addresses the elephant in the room: the key relationship between values, health, and wealth. Understand this, and the rest falls into place naturally."

— SCOTT FULTON
President of Home Ideations LLC
Author of *WHEALTHSPAN: More Years,
More Moments, More Money*

"*Un-Surprise Me!* is not like any other financial book I have ever read. It will help people at any age recognize that they don't have to be victims of their own bad habits. Readers of *Un-Surprise Me!* will be empowered to develop a healthy relationship with money."

— KEVIN NOLAN
Author of *Organizational Muscle*

Un-Surprise Me!

A Fun-Loving Guide for Demystifying Your Financial Future

Jay Wheeler, AIF

modern wisdom
PRESS

modern wisdom
P R E S S

Modern Wisdom Press
Crestone, Colorado, USA
www.ModernWisdomPress.com

Paperback ISBN: 978-1-951692-47-6
eBook ISBN: 978-1-951692-48-3

Cover and interior design by Karen Sperry Graphic Design
Interior author photo courtesy of Chuck Anerino
Back cover author photo courtesy of Dave Shoemaker

To anyone who wants to live a great life
but is unsure how to get there,
You inspire me to support your dreams.

CONTENTS

FOREWORD

This book has helped to explain something that I always thought was a paradox: Why is this fairly educated person, who is facile with numbers in her field, essentially hopeless when those numbers have dollar signs in front of them? Sure, I can balance personal accounts. And I can make basic decisions about the value of one purchase over another or what I can afford. I was even a passable treasurer for a scientific society I belong to. But I just don't have the facility I'd expect of myself with "the big picture," my own overall financial plan. The reason, I learned after reading this book, is that it's not all about the numbers. It's about living "an examined life."

I used to think a personal financial plan consisted of three things:

- Earning money through fulfilling work
- Living within one's means
- Investing by gathering data and applying some basic diversification rules

But perhaps there is more to it. Are the first two the same as working long hours for maximum financial gain and living a life of frugality, whatever the personal cost? Even if we do fine with those, many of us never really succeed at the investing part. We focus on the task intermittently but eventually turn our attention back to other interests, only to find when we check in again that our investments haven't done any better than if we had just left them in a handful of funds.

At the risk of gilding the lily, I think it's fair to say that in this book the author has borrowed timeless ideas from some of Western civilization's greatest thinkers and linked them to the relatively mundane subject of personal finance. What he has produced is a book filled with simple wisdom, a guide to personal financial planning that starts with a process of gaining clarity about one's values, sense of purpose, and sources of true joy.

"Know thyself" quoth the oracle of Delphi—or as author Jay Wheeler would say, "Un-surprise your tendencies."

"The unexamined life is not worth living," observed Socrates in Plato's Apology—or as Jay would say, "Guide yourself."

Surely Jay isn't demanding the depth of philosophical inquiry Socrates was exhorting us to. But he provides valuable guideposts for self-reflection on matters that are most pertinent to how money can be a vehicle for a good life that is consistent with who we are and what we value.

"To thine own self be true," says Polonius in Shakespeare's *Hamlet*—or as Jay would say, "Do it intentionally." Go ahead, be a Maxer if that's who you are. Someone who wants to squeeze all there is out of life and is willing to live with less later, if that's what's consistent with your values or life plan. Or if that scares you to death, and you are one who needs to save for a rainy day to feel safe (what Jay calls a Waiter), that's okay, too. Just be mindful about it and know what it's costing you in quality of life when you're younger. Just be aware of the risks and benefits associated with both approaches to living within one's means.

In this book, the reader is offered exercises in self-reflection and value clarification that press us toward self-knowledge about our own goals, aspirations, and true sources of joy as well as the behavioral tendencies and cognitive biases that can become obstacles on our path to a good life. It provides real-life examples about how mindfulness can help us avoid making consequential decisions about spending and investing money that go against our own self-interest.

This book argues that there is much more to personal financial planning than earning and saving money and managing differences in risk tolerance. Indeed, personal financial planning should be closely coupled with one's life plan. This book not only exhorts us to live an "examined life," it also shows us how decisions we make about money—how we earn it and how we spend it—can serve as a vehicle to realizing our truly transcendent life goals.

— **Judith Jaeger**, PhD
President & Principal Scientist
Cognition Metrics LLC

INTRODUCTION

I was inspired to write this book to help you break down the barriers to being more intentional and effective in planning the precious moments you have in your short time on Earth.

As a financial advisor with 13 years of experience supporting clients of all ages and tax brackets, I will share two realizations I've had in my career.

- The best planning we can do for ourselves transcends financial planning.

- There are simple clues for living a great life all around us that we don't need to be surprised by any longer.

This book will retrain your way of thinking about planning. Finances are just a part of what is needed to live a fulfilling life. If this sounds intimidating, you will find that the opposite is true. Keeping the bigger picture in mind will actually be more satisfying and less intimidating. And with the use of my "hacks," it will be much easier to plan your fulfilling life than you might imagine.

Also, if you're a planning skeptic or avoider, this book offers a flexible approach to accommodate many viewpoints. To help illustrate the importance of planning, I don't hold back from identifying the scarcity of time. The sooner you start planning, the better. I find that leaning in to the limited amount of time and resources we have is a very useful tool to help people take action!

Getting Personal

These are some of my personal motivators for writing *Un-Surprise Me!* for you.

- **To create a relatable guide.** Financial planning can be confusing, so much so that people often avoid it. It breaks my heart when I see people making decisions that are uninformed, overly emotional, or based on false premises. It also pains me to see people make a plan but deviate from it due to a lack of awareness of their own emotional reactions and behavior patterns. We'll work together in the pages of this book to build your clarity and confidence about your life goals and how to achieve them.

- **To offer my expertise in a concise, organized fashion.** I take great pride in the way I explain things to people, and I have been stashing my nuggets and "Jay-isms" into a journal for decades. In this book, you will see an organized compilation of concepts that can make a profound difference in your life. You will experience my friendly approach to teaching you about planning your life—and the means to fund it—as told through client stories, relatable tips, behavioral research, and personal examples.

- **To provide an actionable set of instructions.** Ultimately, I want to inspire you to take action in planning a fulfilling life. I have been on the other side of the desk to hear about a person's situation where it could've been different but it was too late. If you emerge from reading this book feeling more excited, hopeful, and confident that you can take action now to improve your life in a meaningful way, then I've been successful.

- **To take action myself!** I've wanted to write this book for a long time. It's a bucket list thing. And I thought it might inspire you to check something big off your own bucket list. Now that this book is written, I'm immensely proud of it, and I hope it will change some lives. May this inspire you to do something difficult and deeply meaningful. The clock is ticking.

- **To trust in my inner calling.** I felt "called" to write this book, like something wonderful will come from following through on this dream. Maybe you have a calling or a dream that doesn't make sense to your logical mind; you just feel called to do it. And if you do, I hope you'll trust your gut and follow through. We never know where those dreams are leading us until we take action. Life is always calling us to grow.

A Little About Me & My Understanding of You

Wheeler Financial was founded in 2007, with a mission to be a values-driven business and truly put the client first. I took over leadership in 2016, when my father retired from the company. Our practice is committed to balancing the critical advice we give with the dedication to give it in a manner in which the client understands and acts upon it. In fact, we work best with delegators who may be very capable in their own lives but either don't understand or don't want to understand the intricate details of financial planning and investment management. They have the courage to delegate this to a trusted partner.

I've always had a passion for how the mind works and the "human side" of planning. In addition to continuing education on financial planning and investment topics, many of the audiobooks, videos, and podcasts I consume relate to psychology and personal development. I have pursued formal education on the topic of values-based planning in the Behavioral Financial Advice program from think2perform. Additionally, I completed the Behavioral Economics: Consumer Choice and Decision Making program through Wharton Executive Education. I continue to learn about the fine craft of financial advice, as well as learning more about myself and the ways I can be a great advisor to the individuals and families who depend on me.

I don't simply see you as an "investor"; I see you as a fellow human being with dreams, values, and relationships that deeply matter to you. And I know you want to make the right financial decisions.

When you do my job every day, and you do it with empathy, you get an up-close and personal view of the effects that mindset, emotions, and everyday choices have on our life experience.

With your curiosity as you read the pages ahead, I'm going to help you find the clues that are easily accessible to guide you along the life path you hope to follow.

My Research and Writing Style

I am passionate about helping people plan and live better lives by making conscious choices. I've had a wide variety of inspiration, including my training in behavioral finance; my studies of mindfulness, psychology, and self-help; and nuggets from my own life and professional experience.

This book is meant to be entertaining. If I can hold your attention, I can help you make some positive changes in your life. You should also know that I value simplicity, but only to the extent that the core message remains viable.

I have long been inspired by these two quotes:

"Simplicity is the ultimate sophistication."
— inspired by writings from Leonardo da Vinci

"Everything should be made as simple as possible,
but not simpler." — often attributed to Albert Einstein

In our practice, we simplify what can be simplified for the benefit of our clients' understanding, and we pay attention to essential details. During my first five years in the business, I was fortunate to have been trained by my father, who cared *deeply* about the human being behind the portfolio.

He would always say, "Be sure to avoid the three Cs of advice: confuse, complicate, then charge."

In any advice business, there can be a temptation to focus more on justifying the advisor's existence than on solving the client's problems. I'm asking you to embrace a simple, relatable, and even elegant way of planning.

Elegance

I've worked with many coaches and consultants over the years, and a particular concept from a coach named Edwards Holliday significantly shaped our team's way of thinking. He said his goal was to help us to have an "elegant" practice. I didn't initially understand what this meant, as I equated elegance with cocktail attire and ballrooms. I learned that in business, elegance can be defined as combining simplicity and efficiency with sophisticated decisions and outcomes. After a little research, I found that this term is also used in other specific areas of study.

- Math: A formula is *elegant* if it is surprisingly simple and insightful, yet effective and constructive. It uses the fewest number of steps to get to a sophisticated conclusion.

- Pharmacology: *Elegance* in formulation is important for quality as well as for effectiveness in dosage form design, a major component of pharmaceuticals. It delivers the desired therapeutic effect while optimizing dosage and minimizing side effects.

It is entirely possible to simplify your financial planning while still making it deeply meaningful and effective, and I'm excited to share our methods with you.

The most elegant approach to helping our clients build a great life is to do so in a way that transcends financial management. We treat it as a Life Plan, not just a financial plan.

When Billy Joel was a guest on *The Howard Stern Show*, he was asked about his own songs that he didn't like. He said the worst song he had ever written was "We Didn't Start the Fire." He felt it was so poor because he had deviated from his usual songwriting structure of writing the music *first* and then the lyrics.

There are many things in life that don't fit into words… or numbers.

Like your life.

This Life Planning approach can be simpler and more relatable, which can encourage more people to get excited and participate. By identifying the surprises in life that might otherwise trip you up, you make room for the good surprises that may then come your way. This is elegance in action.

Have you thought about what it would take to describe your life as elegant? Would you describe it as elegant now?

Can You Feel It?

It's perfectly okay to talk about emotions when it comes to the topic of money and planning. Yes, we talk about feelings here and also...

- ...your close personal and family relationships and how they can affect your Life Planning.
- ...your common and often predictable behavior patterns.
- ...your history around money.
- ...basically anything in your life experience that is important to you.

I am not a therapist or psychologist, and I don't try to be one. However, when planning, it's critical to address our humanity. I'll help you uncover patterns and decision-making traps. You will identify when it's good to lean on emotion in financial decisions and when it is important to step back from it in favor of solid data when making critical choices.

Searching for Surprises

There are scores of predictable patterns around and within you that can guide your financial planning. Yet most people seem surprised by them. This book will identify these patterns and offer a three-step method for addressing them, so you're not caught off guard.

Isn't the majority of planning for anything just the act of trying to be surprised by fewer things? I have found that under examination, a large portion of our life path can be more predictable than many people could imagine. Once you are trained to uncover the surprises, you will start to connect these dots in everyday life.

There are still "surprise" surprises, of course: COVID, economic downturns, layoffs, war, natural disasters. You will learn how to prepare for those, too.

How to Use This Book

It's best to approach this book with a beginner's mind, forgetting everything you know about financial planning and investments. Get curious about how your life's experiences have programmed you to think about being a consumer, saver, and planner.

At the end of each chapter, you will find exercises called Life-Builders. These are designed to provoke deeper reflection to support, encourage, and challenge you as you build an outline for the future chapters of your life.

When you commit to doing these Life-Builders exercises after you finish each chapter, you can expect impactful and often life-changing results!

I'm excited to share my fun-loving approach to demystifying your financial future. Yes, financial planning can be fun, and it all begins now…so go ahead and dive in!

CHAPTER 1

IT'S TIME TO GET CLARITY

"Life moves pretty fast. If you don't stop and look around once in a while, you could miss it."

— *Ferris Bueller,* Ferris Bueller's Day Off

Because I am a financial advisor, one of the questions I'm often asked from friends and family at dinner parties or on the sidelines of a Little League game is "How do I know if I'm on track?"

Then, as soon as they can tell I'm going to ask a follow-up question, they give a sheepish look as if they might be thinking, *Oh crap, I shouldn't have asked that.* Many people expect me to have a standard answer, but my experience has taught me there isn't one.

First of all, kudos to you for trying to live a great life and wondering whether you are on track. I'm sure you are doing your best.

But what does being "on track" actually mean for you? Seriously. If you told a close friend "I really feel like I'm on track financially, and it feels great!" what exactly would that mean?

Let's start there.

On Track for What?

The "Am I on track?" question usually means that the person wants to know if they are on track for retirement; specifically, whether they will have enough money in their golden years to live decently without additional income. Sometimes it's more, but that's usually about it.

I understand it to be a catch-all question, but there are questions that underlie it, such as...

Is our spending too reckless?

What am I missing out on?

Am I saving too much? Too little?

Should we be helping the kids more? Or less?

What if something happens to one of us?

Could I run out of money?

There are many more, but you get the idea.

And then there are the questions thrust upon us from TV, the internet, or conversations with friends such as...

Could I outlive my assets if I live longer than expected?

What should I do during huge stock market swings?

Should I buy a certain investment product?

Am I handling my 401(k) properly?

And so on.

And even if you figure all that out, does your definition of "on track" consider being able to easily get back on track when life knocks you off the rails, as it sometimes does?

The answer to this question must take into account facets of your upbringing, general life experience, psychology, sociology, and more. I'll attempt to unpack this in the pages ahead, but let's begin with a little story about baggage.

Wants Versus Needs & the Signs of the Rise of Consumption

In 1972, Bernard Sadow received the first US patent for rolling luggage. The idea was hatched after he and his wife struggled with two heavy suitcases while going through customs on the way home from a family vacation in Aruba. The design wasn't perfect, but this innovation was one of many early signs that a shift would eventually happen. In 1987, Northwest Airlines 747 pilot Robert Plath would improve the design, which became the popular Rollaboard we still see in airports today.

Sadow's and Plath's inventions were more than just a convenience. It was foreshadowing of a trend that would eventually take over mindsets in America and then the world. Merely arriving at a destination would no longer be the primary focus. Why drag a big, bulky suitcase around when you can have a better experience in the airport?

The idea of "enjoying the ride" became an area of focus in our culture—and, in many ways, an area of overfocus.

Now suitcases with wheels are everywhere. We went from not knowing about a certain convenience to wanting it, and now it feels like a true need. And this extends to numerous other products that have been upgraded and gotten more expensive. A simple cup of coffee has become a $5.95 venti latte, Little League went to travel sports, smartphones cost $1,000 or more—and countless other luxuries have become must-haves in our daily lives.

There has been a generational shift from valuing frugality and security to one where opportunities for consumption are seemingly everywhere, and the prevailing opinion seems to be to "live more for the present moment."

There is also societal pressure to consume. For example, kids are being encouraged to attend college more than in previous generations, and the cost of universities has skyrocketed.

Don't get me wrong—I enjoy many of these material things and experiences myself, and Lindsay and I plan to send our kids to good colleges. But we understand this comes at a cost.

So how do we make sense of it all?

Part of your new "Am I on track?" question could be "How much of 'enjoying the ride' is the right amount, and at what cost?"

But first, there is an important factor at play that may explain why many people keep chasing a ballooning lifestyle, and it's important for you to understand how it may be affecting you.

The Cost of Fleeting Happiness

That smiling Amazon box of goodies you were so excited about when you ordered them is now sitting on your front step, full of expiring happiness, and something called hedonic adaptation is to blame.

Hedonic adaptation describes our psychological tendency to return to our own baseline level of happiness relatively quickly, even after significant positive or negative experiences. This phenomenon suggests that the long-term effect of external changes is less than we may think.

Think of hedonic adaptation as a happiness thermostat that regulates your emotions, in the same way as your house thermostat regulates the temperature. Studies show that after time, the feelings surrounding very positive or very negative events tend to diminish, and a person returns to a level near their baseline happiness.

Hedonic adaptation explains why…

- That new car gets less appealing after a while.
- Lottery winners often struggle after a short-term spike in happiness.
- Your twenty-fifth year of marriage, while it may be great, is different than your honeymoon.

The happiness thermostat is reset with time and comes back to the baseline. Then people set out to seek another "hit" of happiness.

Hedonic adaptation also explains the saying "Time heals all wounds." I suppose time doesn't heal all wounds, but it changes the intensity enough so that people can focus on other things and resume a relatively normal life. An awareness of this can affect your financial decisions by allowing you to take a mindful pause from reactionary spending when dealing with a challenging situation.

Understanding hedonic adaptation can feel empowering. It explains why experiences and purchases can have a short-term effect on our happiness but may not have a lasting one.

Later, we'll dive into the question "How much does a feeling cost?" I will show you a way to identify how much you spend on various feelings such as happiness and security, and you'll learn how to determine which ones are worth investing in.

Balancing Spending and Saving

It's important to note here that challenges related to consumption are not limited to common present-day overconsumption. While I would say we see more cases of overconsumption than underconsumption, we must also sometimes address over-savings. In fact, some of the stories that stick with me the most are ones where people have been overly frugal. I wish they had learned a more balanced approach, including more spending on things that were meaningful to them. Two examples come to mind.

Earlier in my career, I worked with a wonderful older couple. There were very frugal, especially the husband. As a result, they had built up quite a large investment portfolio. Sadly, the husband passed away after a long battle with an illness.

A few weeks after the funeral, I met with the wife. Almost immediately, she started crying. "We don't need all this money! I wish we had traveled more and done more adventurous things together. We have all this money, and it really means nothing to me."

This interaction reaffirmed my commitment to helping clients find the ideal saving and spending balance that is right for them and facilitate communication around these topics. If only she had been this open when we'd first connected years earlier, maybe their lives would have been full of amazing experiences together.

In a situation with a different result, another couple was also very frugal and had saved quite a bit of money. They had inherited a beach house, which was split with the husband's brother.

After working together for a while, I asked him, "What would you wish for, if money were no object?"

He said, "An addition to the beach house. It's my dream to expand on our wonderful family getaway, which has been the home of so many great memories for all of us."

It took them five years, but after careful budgeting, values exercises, and deep conversations, they finally took the plunge. I'll admit I got a little choked up when he told me this addition was something his father had dreamed of, but he'd passed away before he could do it. That almost happened to these clients, too, but instead they made a great educated consumption choice that was meaningful to them and their family.

Finding Abundance from Scarcity

Our time on Earth is short, and ignoring that is a huge mistake. Obsessing about it is, too. I believe that it's critical to address the scarcity of time when planning. When done correctly, it can actually create abundance for the amazing opportunity we have to be alive right now.

In his article "The Tail End" in the *Wait But Why* blog, author Tim Urban does an excellent job of illustrating our remaining lifetime by using experiences instead of days, months, or years. Through relatable examples such as vacations, Super Bowls, and even calculating the number of pizzas he will likely eat in his remaining life, Urban hits us with the scarcity of our time remaining to do things. It's striking when we measure our life in moments, not minutes.

Here are some examples.

- For a person aged 65 who loves the beach and goes for a week once per year, they may have 20 or fewer trips remaining, depending on their health and longevity.

- If you have one really wonderfully deep conversation per year with an 80-year-old parent, there is a significant chance that your remaining number of these meaningful discussions could be in the single digits.

- A big fan of the Winter Olympics who is 50 may only be able to see their favorite curling event about eight more times, give or take.

- If you have a best friend who lives far away, and you're only able to visit them once every five years…

Well, you get the math. As parents of two wonderful kids in their teens, my wife Lindsay and I are keenly focused on making the most of every moment with them before they head to college. By the time children turn 12, a parent has typically already spent about 75% of their total in-person time together.

Make these interactions happen, and make them count.

To do this, you will need to find a balance: how much to work, how much to play, how much to spend, and how much to save. You will be chasing a great lifestyle, but how much is too much?

Is All of This Chasing Worth It?

There is a quote attributed to author Edgar Alan Moss that goes "How many people do you know who are spending money they have not yet earned for things they don't need to impress people they don't like?"

This quote comes from Moss's syndicated column "Office Cat" in 1929. I have a feeling Mr. Moss would be horrified to see how his question would be answered these days.

For many people, their wants…

   …have become needs…

   …which have become handcuffs…

   …to a pricey lifestyle…

   …with them working really hard at the office and at home to try to manage it all.

But before we give up on all of our goals around material things and travel, some of this consumption is truly enjoyable and worth the chase.

Upon examination, some of it may not be. Yet we keep chasing it.

In a Deloitte survey of 1,000 professionals, 77% of respondents cited that they had felt burnout at their current job, and more than half said they had felt this feeling multiple times during their lifetime. And while the survey focused on workplace conditions leading to burnout, so many people have lifestyles that force them to work long hours in higher-paying jobs to make it all work.

I certainly have no issue with hard work. What disheartens me is to see people chasing a lifestyle that is either unintentional or hasn't been properly thought out.

I work hard at my job, sometimes long hours, but I set it up so that it is in service of the Life Plan my wife and I have created together. We are very clear about what we want, and we have really good conversations with each other about that. I check in with myself often, and Lindsay too, to ensure that the significant time I'm working is in service of something specific and important.

The chapters ahead will help teach you how to develop this level of intentionality in a way that works for you.

Why People Don't Plan

It's okay to get a little bit of a pukey feeling when the subject of planning comes up.

There are many legitimate reasons people choose not to plan, and this can be based on psychological, practical, and emotional factors. Following are some reasons people are resistant to planning. Underneath each one, I have included ideas for how you can manage them.

- **Fear of Commitment:** Many of us link planning with locking ourselves into a specific course of action. This can feel intimidating and uncomfortable.

We all have varying history with how life has programmed us to feel about commitment, and that's okay. If this is an issue for you, ask yourself if it has served to protect you or not. Building awareness of the source of this pattern and the possible costs of avoiding commitment can help you stick to a plan.

- **Perceived Loss of Flexibility:** Many people value spontaneity, and they feel that nailing down too many things can restrict their freedom to live freely. Planning can be seen as limiting the ability to adapt to changing circumstances.

Identify what you might lose with planning. Also, be specific about the feelings you gained through this flexibility, and whether they generally outweigh the results you get with more intentional behavior. Make a simple rule for yourself about when you will stick to your plan and when you will deviate—without judging yourself for it.

- **Fear of Failure:** If you have perfectionistic tendencies or you highly value achievement, you may avoid setting a plan with specific expected outcomes. It's not uncommon to avoid planning altogether if you are uneasy about living up to the expectations you may set for yourself.

Your plan is not a competition. It is a way of guiding you to something that you want right now. You could start getting close to achieving a goal and realize it's not something you wanted after all. Or your plan might "fail" but lead to something even better. If a fear of failure is underlying your resistance, it's probably worth exploring this more deeply, perhaps with the help of a trained therapist.

- **Overwhelm and Anxiety:** In planning, you are dealing with an uncertain future, and you are sometimes forced to consider unappealing outcomes. Even the idea of things being out of your control can feel uncomfortable. This anxiety can increase with the level of complexity in planning.

  Mindfulness can be helpful here. A period of meditation and intention-setting before you start to plan can be useful. If the anxiety persists, just try to be with that sensation in the body and see if there is anything you can learn from it. Also, make it simple. Start with something that is meaningful and achievable. As you rack up some planning wins, celebrate them.

- **Procrastination:** It's totally normal to delay uncomfortable tasks. Procrastination can come from a variety of sources. Part of the issue is not knowing how to begin.

  Get curious about your patterns of procrastination. What is the cost of putting things off right now? (Be specific.) What tends to end your procrastination? This book will provide a planning system that is less intimidating, thus alleviating your hesitation to begin.

- **Lack of Skills:** Financial planning comes naturally to a small group of people, but for most, it requires new skills. Until people develop those, planning can be intimidating.

  There is a method for nearly everything, and in the pages of this book, you will learn some simple tips to feel more confident.

- **Past Negative Experiences:** Many people have been scarred by an overbearing parent or boss who forced their method of financial planning on them. These wounds can be deep. People can also be hesitant based on past plans that didn't go as expected.

  Think about how your life experiences have affected your feelings about financial planning. What positives can you find from this? Are there areas where you need to find forgiveness and move on?

- **Social Factors:** Research shows that there can be variation among groups and cultures, where some enjoy living in the moment more than others. And many families reject planning in favor of spontaneity.

  Think about how these social factors may have affected your feelings about planning. Jot down which of these have served you well, and also make note of the areas that have served you poorly. Decide which beliefs you wish to retain and which you are ready to let go.

If you have an aversion to financial planning, seek out the root of these feelings. This self-awareness will make this process much easier.

The Answer to "Am I on Track?"

I spent a good portion of my life chasing accomplishments and experiences, and then immediately upon achievement, I would move on to chase something new. Nothing was ever enough. Through maturity and personal development, I'm no longer caught in that trap as much, and I'm more at peace with that part of me. But I had to go there to get here.

I now have a very detailed idea of the lifestyle we want to have as a family, and the legacy I would like to create personally and professionally. With a framework for identifying, winning, and *celebrating*, I have found a greater degree of satisfaction.

Does this sound familiar? Do you know what you are chasing? Would you be satisfied if you got it? Then what?

It's critical to have a system for consumption and also a system for satisfaction.

It's time for you to reinvent your "on track" question with something more personal and targeted. In the pages ahead, you will set a foundation for the life you want to live.

And you'll do this by...

- Readjusting the lens through which you plan your life.
- Finding more intentionality in your spending and saving choices.
- Determining your financial goals in a way you can understand and act upon.
- Planning a financial approach that is bigger and more impactful than simple goal-setting.
- Learning how to be aware of information that should not be surprising at all.
- Identifying your own behavior traps that could derail you.

- Communicating effectively with your partner about life and money.
- Living in a spirit of abundance and acceptance while embracing imperfection.

This book will give you the ability to skillfully do more by doing less.

Have you ever seen a group of older guys play basketball against ripped, physically fit high schoolers or college kids? Initially, the youngsters will impress the audience with feats of athleticism and hustle. There are dunks and fancy plays, with lots of movement and dribbling. Meanwhile, when the old guys get the ball, it almost looks like they aren't even trying. This is because they are utilizing their experience and not wasting energy on things that are not important. Their passes, shots, and subtle tricks are much more *intentional*, and they don't waste movement. They can't afford to! Over the course of the game, the youngsters get worn out from chasing the intentional movements of the older guys.

Living the "How do I know if I'm on track?" life can take too much energy and wear you out. The On-Purpose Method® you'll learn about in the upcoming chapters leans on your life experience to figure out your next move.

Behavioral Finance

When our son, Grady, was young, I bet we watched bits and pieces of the Disney movie *Cars* with him no less than 100 times. It was his favorite. I love the part where Hudson Hornet, the older, more experienced race car, teaches young racer Lightning McQueen about the value of counter-steering, which is where a driver will "turn left to go right" around the curves of a racetrack.

The answer to your "Am I on track?" question just may be found by turning left to go right. Instead of leaning into your financial life and making that the primary focus, as many of us have been trained to do, I'm suggesting that the investments, account selection, and savings plan should be some of the very *last* things you do.

There are many reasons for this, one of which is that financial management is unpleasant for many people. Another is that if we are in a rush to make financial decisions, we often skip over the reasons for them. You can make higher-quality investment decisions as a result of your increased awareness and vision of the future. While it may seem counterintuitive, you're adding value by allowing this essential part of your planning to develop.

By using a behavioral approach where finance and psychology intersect, we emphasize the human factors that affect both your life and your money.

"I've Lived a Great Life"

A client in his eighties named Joe and I were wrapping up an annual planning meeting in my office one day.

He turned to me and said, "You know, Jay, I've lived a great life."

This struck me and stuck with me.

Have you ever said that? "I've lived a great life."

If not, what would it take for you to say that?

Before you read any further, start saying it right now…and say it often.

You have done your best, and you will continue to do your best. Sure, it's not perfect. But by saying "I'm living a great life," you just may find a greater degree of abundance that will affect your wants, and corresponding spending and behavior, in surprising ways.

Next, let's dive into the story of how I was awakened to the value of the "human side" of money and planning. It has become my intention to identify and solve the many ways people spend much of their lives being surprised by things that can be avoided or easily planned for.

Life-Builders

To build a solid foundation, you must get clarity on both your current situation and the life you want to live. Below, you will find some questions to explore about your work and personal life. Write your answers in a notebook or journal. Be honest with yourself, because this is the first step in knowing whether you are on the right track.

1. On a scale of 1 to 10, how hard do you currently work at your job? (Factor in both hours and stress.)
    VERY LITTLE 1 2 3 4 5 6 7 8 9 10 WAY TOO MUCH

2. In 20 years, will you feel that you worked a healthy amount this year?
    NOT AT ALL 1 2 3 4 5 6 7 8 9 10 ABSOLUTELY!

3. Do you tend to spend money on experiences now or save for later?
    SAVE FOR LATER 1 2 3 4 5 6 7 8 9 10 SPEND IT NOW

4. List at least five things you spend a lot of money on that you feel are worth your hard work and job stress.

5. What are three examples of material things or experiences you work really hard to attain but might not be worth the long hours of work or large expense?

6. Schedule time to have a conversation with your partner about planning for the future. Before you meet, each of you should make a list of items and experiences that are important as well as your desired outcome from the conversation.

BUILD A ~~FINANCIAL~~ LIFE

I've been aware of the scarcity of time from a young age. I think this began with an experience I had with my grandfather, Jim Porter, who was my very first fishing buddy.

During his career, Pop Pop (as I called him) worked as a fore-man for Sun Oil Company (now known as Sunoco) at their refinery in Marcus Hook, Pennsylvania. In the evenings, he worked as an artist for Happy Harry's drugstore and designed their logo, which has surprisingly popped back in fashion over the past several years.

When I was about 11, Pop Pop and I were scheduled to go on a fishing trip in the Delaware Bay with his neighbor Mr. Svaab, a nice man with a beautiful fishing boat. This trip was a real treat, so I was *really* looking forward to it!

I remember saying to Pop Pop, "I am so excited for the trip! I wish today was Friday."

And then, Pop Pop gave me a surprisingly stern look, which was out of character for him. He said, "Jay, don't wish your life away! Enjoy every day for what it is."

The message really stuck with me. As a kid, I thought I was in trouble for saying the wrong thing, but I've learned more about those words over time. As I look back on it as an adult, I realize Pop Pop was aging; he would eventually suffer from a prolonged illness. It comforts me to know that he never wished his life away, and his mantra powers much of the advice I give my financial clients today. It has truly shaped my life view, both personally and professionally.

To give you an idea of how this story impacted my career destiny, I want to share a bit of my professional background so you'll learn how this message became an integral part of our business today.

Why I Didn't Become a Financial Advisor

My dad started working as a financial advisor in 1986. He often told us stories at the dinner table of the families he was helping and the interesting situations they found themselves in. It was a job he loved. It evolved from an occupation to more like a vocation for him, and he took tremendous pride in the recommendations he gave to his clients. My dad tried other careers before eventually finding his love of providing financial advice for people.

Fast-forward to 2004, when Lindsay and I were engaged, and I was contemplating a career change after chasing my dream of working in professional sports. I had worked in the front offices of franchises in the NBA, NHL, and AHL. I had some proud accomplishments working in pro sports, but it was time to find a job consistent with the family lifestyle Lindsay and I wanted to live. My dad suggested I consider the financial advice business, which had worked well for him for so many years.

I had some meetings and interviews with the large firm he worked with at the time, and I did significant research. I met with management and spent some time in the office to get a sense of what working in finance would be like.

I really *wanted* to like it. There were a lot of bright people in that business, and working with numbers was something I always enjoyed. But something didn't feel right to me.

It reminds me of how I feel about drinking scotch. I like the idea of having a nice glass of it, but I just don't like the taste.

At that time, the business was mostly built around the commission-based selling of investments. I certainly don't mean to disparage anyone who was in the business at that time. Many advisors helped people make significantly more money than they would have made on their own. But I didn't want to be a stockbroker.

Being a stockbroker, or what was then starting to be called a financial advisor, just didn't feel like me. I couldn't put my finger on it at the time. It would take me years to figure out why. (More on that later.)

So I decided not to enter the financial business. But I was still left with a decision to make: I needed a new career.

I noticed that the home improvement business was not known for being too customer-friendly, and I wondered if I could pair my passion for building with my skills of providing great service.

In what was probably my worst business decision ever, I started a home remodeling business. Over the next several years, we did some really nice projects, and I met some great people, but it was hard. I discovered that the difficult client experience in home improvement was partially a product of the intricacies of coordinating subcontractors, clients, municipalities, and more.

It was also incredibly hard on my body; my back will never be the same. I have tremendous respect for my friends in that field who continue to run successful businesses. But after several years, I started to realize I didn't want to do it forever.

Why I Did Become a Financial Advisor

It was November 2010, and I was working long hours, struggling and unhappy after years in the home remodeling business. As it turns out, my dad was grappling with a decision of his own. He was 64 and needed a succession plan for his business.

A few years earlier, he had taken his financial planning practice independent under the name Wheeler Financial, and he knew it would eventually need new leadership, as he planned to retire in 2016, at age 70.

The business had evolved to include an increased focus on financial planning, and the values my dad had instilled in Wheeler Financial really got me excited about how I could help people. Financial planning software had come a long way, and the techniques being used were making more of a difference in people's lives than ever. Additionally, he affiliated Wheeler Financial with Raymond James Financial, and their client-centric values made for an amazing relationship between the two organizations.

I took the plunge and began the process of becoming licensed as a financial advisor and learning the business. I was excited to build my skills so I could capably take over for my dad and handle the tremendous responsibility of helping people manage their financial lives.

I spent the first few years of my career as a financial advisor learning the ropes. Within five years, I was in charge of helping about 200 families manage their life savings.

The pressure was on.

During that time, I had the good fortune of being mentored by my dad. He truly cares about other people, and I am so fortunate to have inherited that trait from both of my parents. I learned how to treat our clients well while gaining a tremendous amount of technical knowledge.

My dad is a longtime believer in financial planning and a true student of the game. His investment process, later named the On-Purpose Method, is the one we continue to use in our practice today.

As time went on and I became a capable advisor, I prepared to take over our company and purchase Wheeler Financial. It just so happened that Lindsay and I had found a perfect house right around that time, and settlement for it would be on the Friday before our Wheeler Financial settlement. Over those several days, I borrowed more money than I will probably ever borrow again in my life. There was a lot on the line, especially since we now had two young children.

As the new leader of Wheeler Financial, I wanted to apply my own authentic style to the business. What did I bring to our clients that was unique, and how did I discover it?

The Puzzle-Solving Advisor

It didn't take me long as a financial advisor to realize that in addition to being a strategist, a significant part of my role would be as a teacher explaining complex topics to clients in a relatable way.

I am quite good at puzzle games and seeing patterns, so I could envision a financial plan like a puzzle of sorts. There are so many different variables, and I got really excited about seeing how we could fit the pieces together in a way that was right for each client. We spent hours looking at account contribution and withdrawal strategies, related asset allocation, tax management, and so much more.

After a while, I realized that the puzzle included a lot more than investments or financial plans. Some pieces of the puzzle were missing!

I began to see behavioral patterns that impacted financial decisions, such as how we might react (and spend money) after a crappy day at work. Most of us know that "retail therapy" isn't a very smart practice. I saw how people's health decisions could impact their future retirement. Missing pieces to the puzzle included relationship dynamics with loved ones, overall well-being, and conditioned behavior that people learn growing up.

This puzzle was bigger than a mere financial plan; it was a Life Plan.

Other puzzle pieces are right there in front of you, but you may not notice them. These are the avoidable "surprises" you'll learn more about in the pages to follow.

I saw how I could bring a unique approach to teaching our clients how to make solid decisions around their life through the use of mindfulness.

A Breath of Fresh Air

About 15 years ago, I started dabbling in meditation to manage stress. This interest grew relatively quickly, but like many people new to this practice, I found it difficult and frustrating. I eventually enrolled in a course called Mindfulness-Based Stress Reduction (MBSR), and I saw some significant breakthroughs in my practice.

Mindfulness is a form of meditation that you can bring into your everyday activities, essentially helping you become less attached to your thoughts and emotions and more present in your moment-by-moment experience.

I've always found value in doing difficult things. Whether I was completing triathlons such as the Escape from Alcatraz and the Syracuse Iron Man 70.3 or tackling the 75 Hard Challenge or something else, I love pushing myself. But MBSR was harder. Being alone with your thoughts is hard work! In fact, in his mindfulness book *10% Happier*, former *Nightline* anchor Dan Harris joked that his alternative title for the book was *The Voice in My Head Is an A**hole*, but network executives wouldn't allow it.

Whether you have a mindfulness practice is up to you, and we don't push it with our clients. Yet a primary goal of this book is to help you create more self-awareness and follow through on your Life Plan. And the practice of mindfulness can help you "protect yourself from yourself."

Mindfulness will help you…

- **Respond, not react.** One of the many benefits to a mindfulness practice is becoming aware of emotions and responses. My meditation practice gives me an added split second of awareness in the moment. In our recommendations, we help to make clients mindful of factors at play in their spending and saving decisions.

- **Let go of judgment.** An increased awareness of everything that is going on at a certain time naturally fosters more compassion. We begin to make decisions and choices *with less judgment* of our thoughts or emotions around them. In working with clients, I aim to help them use their emotions to their advantage, and part of that is not judging how they feel.

- **Embrace uncertainty and change.** Mindfulness helps us to see that things are always changing and will eventually end. This applies to the good, the bad, and everything in between.

  - *The good:* As I noted earlier, positive feelings associated with a new purchase are often fleeting. We can get emotional about the excitement around a new purchase, and often we can become very good salespeople for ourselves—sometimes too good. By providing gentle reminders that a purchase may not be the solution to all of life's problems, we sometimes help people make better decisions.

- *The not-so-good:* Knowing that change is inevitable also applies to the challenging situations in life. They, too, come to an end…or at least become less painful. This lesson has helped me comfort clients during difficult circumstances.

These are just a few areas where mindfulness can lead to improved decisions.

Because of my own mindfulness journey, I knew it was time to commit to our Life Planning methods once and for all. Soon after I purchased Wheeler Financial in 2016, we gradually began to introduce behavioral and mindfulness concepts as part of our advice.

Breaking Up with the Advisor I Thought I Was Supposed to Be

We took the plunge and spent a big chunk of money remodeling our office's main client meeting room. It now has a really comfy, updated look along with some cutting-edge technology, including a 75-inch touchscreen that clients and advisors can use to manipulate and annotate on our financial planning software.

But included in the design was something that both wildly excited me and absolutely terrified me at the same time. Emblazoned on the wall in large letters, there is a sign that reads:

LIFE DESIGN STUDIO

Our team and I had pushed in all of our cards on our Life Planning approach. We wanted to have this on the wall to remind ourselves and our clients of Wheeler Financial's commitment to the Life Plan. We are unapologetic about not making financial planning the "main thing." This was also my way of saying that

I was letting go of the advisor I thought I was supposed to be and adding our own spin to the traditional financial advisor training I had received.

Initially, I just dipped my toe in and started lightly dripping behavioral concepts on clients. The feedback was excellent. The next big step was to implement values-based planning, and we've seen some really cool breakthroughs as a result. Even now, I wonder how much I can push the envelope with the behavioral approach, but the more we do it, the better the feedback gets.

It's now time for you to take your own steps forward as you learn about our Life Planning process. Read along and explore what you can learn about your tendencies, values, and patterns around money and life.

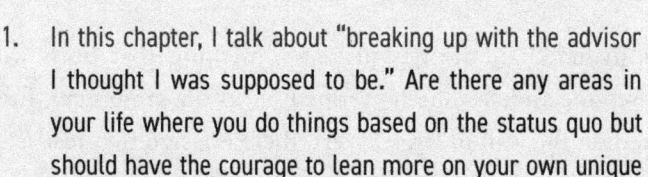

Life-Builders

1. In this chapter, I talk about "breaking up with the advisor I thought I was supposed to be." Are there any areas in your life where you do things based on the status quo but should have the courage to lean more on your own unique approach? List each of them.

2. Mindfulness helps to cultivate the ability to thoughtfully respond instead of quickly reacting. What are some areas of your life where you might benefit by taking this approach?

CHAPTER 3

ILLUMINATING
THE ON-PURPOSE METHOD®

"Plans are of little importance, but planning is essential."
— *Winston Churchill*

What is financial planning, anyway? As you read this section, I ask you to let go of anything you believe about planning or any excess baggage you might have around this topic.

Imagine that planning was nothing more than the act of...

- Avoiding or preparing for certain surprises or unintended outcomes.

- Steering your future in a particular direction.

That's it.

Give yourself permission to let go of some of the uneasy feelings you have about financial planning for a moment. If you view it as simply trying to identify the things you might be surprised by and then directing yourself on an intentional path, you may find that the future seems less hectic.

Let's dive deeper into the idea of avoiding surprises or unintended outcomes and being prepared for them.

To oversimplify it, let's say you wake up for work and you check the weather. Just by doing that, you are planning! Some people would be surprised by a downpour that day, but you won't be.

I'm simply suggesting that you "check the weather" in more areas of your life. And I'm going to show you how.

Steer Your Future in a Particular Direction

Whether conscious or unconscious, intentional or unintentional, we are continuously making choices. With just a few small adjustments, you will increase your confidence that the life you've always wanted to live may actually happen after all.

I realize that people have varying opinions about planning ahead and seeking to control outcomes. And we'll get to that in a moment. But first, let's take a look at how certain life events can play "peekaboo" at inopportune times.

Object Permanence & Your Financial Plan

As a student at the University of Delaware, I took a course in early childhood development.

The main reason I took the class was that I was the only male student in the classroom, but I actually learned a lot of very interesting things that have helped me become a more well-rounded person and parent.

One of the most interesting concepts we learned in this course was the development of object permanence, a major milestone in the first year of life. It means that the child knows that an object or person *continues to exist* once it moves out of their line of sight.

According to Swiss psychologist Jean Piaget, known for his research on childhood development, infants typically learn object permanence at about the age of eight months. This explains why a younger baby may drop a toy, but because they can no longer see it, they don't look for it. It also explains why young children love the game of peekaboo. Infants younger than about eight months perceive you as literally disappearing and reappearing. (I would probably laugh, too! Great party trick.)

How is the idea of object permanence relevant to your planning?

In a similar way, important information can fade into the background when we make major decisions. I frequently see people allow certain financial obligations to "disappear." Here's an example.

A couple decides to splurge on a big, expensive family vacation. They have justified all the reasons they deserve to take the trip. But as soon as they make the final payment for the trip… PEEKABOO! Their HVAC system has a catastrophic failure and needs to be replaced to the tune of $14,000.

They just got surprised by something that shouldn't be surprising…kind of like a baby does.

That HVAC system was 22 years old. But using our planning method, this couple could have avoided the stress that will come with the situation as they scramble to find the needed funds.

Many people don't look hard enough at the big picture, so much of their planning is short-term focused.

But before you get into finding the unsurprising surprises in your life, you need to consider exactly what you are trying to plan for and how to approach it.

Planning Your One Precious Life

My career as a financial advisor has certainly changed the lens through which I view life. I get to be with clients for the planning and the victories, which is intensely rewarding. On the other hand, we also work with our clients right up until the end of life, and we work with their loved ones afterward.

I will never take my responsibility for granted. It has changed me forever.

Maintaining close relationships with clients right up until the end has made me very sensitive to the fragility of life and the scarcity of time. Life is short, and it's shorter for some than for others. I take personal responsibility for challenging people to imagine what's possible for them within the limits of their resources and time.

My breakthrough happened when, through my own choice and with the support of my coworkers and family, I started to teach what I knew in my heart was the best way to approach this business: to respect and fully address the technical matters of financial planning and investment management, but also to *treat the process as the holistic Life Plan that it is.*

During the process of planning your life together, we discover behavior patterns that may be getting in the way and address them fully so you can successfully carry out that plan. One of those limiting behaviors is avoiding the financial part.

Avoiding Planning Avoidance

I frequently think about the door to our office, about the jitters people have as they walk through it. I get a lot of apologies about the nervousness people feel. "I'm sorry, I know I'm supposed to be more on top of this. It's just not my thing." Many people view a financial office as a den of jargon, complexity, and shame…with a lot at stake.

It's okay if financial planning sucks for you. Good news—it doesn't for me. I love it!

I don't apologize to my doctor about not knowing the inner workings of the human body, and I don't apologize to my mechanic for not knowing how to service the engine in my car. So you don't need to apologize for not knowing all the details of your financial life. You don't do this every day like financial advisors do.

When you say, "I'm going to start my Life Planning now, and I will work on the financial details later," it takes a lot of the pressure off. Developing your dreams and aspirations can actually be fun, and it will lead you to the important financial part eventually.

The History of Over-Financing

Only since about the year 2000 has it become increasingly acceptable to talk publicly about behavior or mental health. And it was certainly not cool to do so in the world of finance. Until recently, talk of Life Planning may have been considered "fluffy" and certainly not scientific.

A generation or so ago, financial advisors, who were mostly considered stockbrokers, focused on helping people buy and sell securities to make more money. People are drawn to the idea of making money, especially that rush that comes along with a steep increase in market value.

Then there was a gradual rise in financial planning. This provided valuable insight for clients who were interested in preparing for certain goals, particularly retirement. But in many ways, investment and account selection have remained a primary focus in our industry.

Rather than creating a financial plan aimed at living a great life, create a great Life Plan with strong financial management as one of your many tools to drive that forward.

During the 2000s, we have seen the rise of behavioral finance, where psychology and finance intersect. And it's truly wonderful. The idea that our profession is focusing more on the emotions that drive behavior behind the portfolio is groundbreaking. However, there is still more work to do. Even with an increased focus on behavioral concerns, it often still comes back to the money part. Many behavioral finance approaches consider behavior to the extent that it affects people's investment choices. A common approach is to outline the cognitive biases that cause people to abandon their investment plans.

Much of the training and messaging in our industry leads us to believe that money is the "main thing." There are many brilliant financial advisors out there, and tremendous advice is given every day. I would love to see that continue, with the addition of this more human approach that would have a profound impact on the client.

The reasons for over-financing are not limited to our industry's professionals. Far too often, clients are motivated by the gambler mentality of the big win in the stock market and don't focus enough on the daily changes they can make in their choices, which often have a much bigger impact on their end results than security selection.

Your Dreams Don't Care About Your Roth IRA

"Here lies Jay. He was financially efficient."

That's not what I'm going for. That's part of it, but it's far from the main thing.

Rather than creating a financial plan aimed at living a great life, create a great Life Plan with strong financial management as one of your many tools to drive that forward.

The method of financial planning traditionally used is, in my opinion, simply a mix-up of strategy and tactics.

When making any plan…

- Strategy is the WHAT.
- Tactics are the HOW.

Strategy serves to guide the actions you should take to get the outcome you want. The strategy is *to do the things that it takes to live a great life*. That's the big thing.

Beneath that, tactics include creating a smart financial plan, but that's not all. They also include things like a plan for healthy living, strong relationships, and amazing experiences. There are lots of tactics, but they all point to this outcome of trying to have a great life.

Where you start matters. Do you see how results can be different by creating a life strategy instead of a financial strategy?

A money-first approach is like planning a great day on the lake and letting your boat mechanic plan it for you. Nothing against boat mechanics, but there's a lot more to that plan than just your boat. Granted, if it breaks down, you won't have a day on the lake, but there is a lot more work that goes into planning an amazing lake day, like deciding who to spend it with, what to bring, and what to eat.

Illuminating What's Obvious

Sometimes we look in the wrong place for what we need.

The drunkard's search principle, also known as the "streetlight effect," describes a common observational bias that can affect our decision-making and planning. The name is derived from a fable that goes like this:

> A police officer was responding to a call about an intoxicated male. When the officer arrived at the scene, he saw a drunken individual searching for something under a streetlight. When the police officer asked what the man was looking for, he replied that he had lost his keys. The officer then joined in trying to help him find the lost keys in the area of the streetlight. After several minutes, the officer asked the man if he was sure he lost them in that location.

The man responded, "No, I lost them in the park."

The officer said, "Then why are we looking here?"

"Because this is where the light is," the drunk man said.

The officer shook his head, got out his flashlight, and walked over to the park, where they quickly found the lost keys.

The drunkard's search principle says that people tend to search for something where it is easiest to look.

In the chapters ahead, you are going to look at certain areas of your life that can be "lost keys" and then easily organize them so they will be "right under the streetlight." Certain parts of your future will become much more obvious once we illuminate them.

You Are Special but Probably Not Unique

In my early days at Wheeler Financial, my dad proudly showed me what he called a "considerations" page. It was brilliant. He broke people down into simple age-based groups and then listed the common financial factors they should be thinking about based on their situation.

For example, when a person is in their twenties in what we call the "accumulation phase," they are typically acquiring things like a car, a house, furniture, and dishes. There are a specific set of unsurprising considerations that uniquely apply to people in this phase of life that don't apply later. Then we have mid-career considerations, where people may be having kids and moving forward in their careers. Different considerations apply to people in pre-retirement and retirement phases.

So while you are unique in some ways, you should identify the areas in which you are typical for others in your stage of life. I'm going to turn you into a sleuth for the surprisingly obvious.

To view the important considerations at various stages of life, visit www.WheelerFinancial-llc.com/life_stages.

Doing It on Purpose

Here is where we start to build your life together. There are three primary steps you will take to create a plan for an intentional, thoughtful, and values-driven life. It's called the On-Purpose Method.

1. Know yourself.

2. Guide yourself.

3. Protect yourself (mainly from yourself).

In the chapters that follow, you will learn more about these three steps to crafting a thoughtful, creative, and personalized plan. This approach will break down the barriers of fear and perfectionism that often stop people from planning at all. But for now, here is some basic information for each step.

STEP 1: Know yourself.

In many current planning approaches, little thought is given to effective goal-setting. The result is a good plan that executes poorly constructed goals. Before making a plan to achieve your goals, you must ensure that they are the right ones for you in the context of who you are and the life you want to live. You achieve this by considering your general tendencies and values, and by being intentional.

Tendencies: There is tremendous value in taking a step back and building an awareness of your decision-making tendencies. These can come from your belief system, your parents' belief systems, or other aspects of your upbringing. A mindful awareness of these tendencies often results in making better choices.

Values: Values-driven goals ensure that they align with your core beliefs and what you consider essential. In Chapter 5, you will learn about an exercise to identify the personal values you want to prioritize. You will learn how to use these to both evaluate your current life and to make strong decisions moving forward.

Intentionality: Once you have a clear idea of your values and the life you desire, you should be intentional about your planning. I will teach you how to do this effectively. When you commit to moving forward with intentionality toward your desired end results, you can start to put together a plan for achieving those goals.

STEP 2: Guide yourself.

Remember, in planning you essentially need to…

- Avoid surprises or unintended outcomes.
- Steer your future in a particular direction.

In this section, we will take a deep dive into your life's "surprises." This includes gathering relevant data and beginning to manage your financials.

Data: In the absence of data, your emotions take over your financial planning. By following our approach, you will learn how to use your data in a way that is not intimidating...and less unpleasant.

Financial Management: We finally get to the investments! Once you get there, you will see the value in moving the money focus from the beginning of the planning process to the end. This way, there can be considerably more thoughtfulness in account selection, withdrawal strategies, and investment allocation.

STEP 3: Protect yourself (mainly from yourself).

Awareness of Your Behavior Patterns: Just as you will un-surprise other parts of your life, there is tremendous value in understanding your behavior patterns. Once you have put together this great Life Plan, you need to be in a good position to carry it out. The first step in doing this is to notice your typical behavior patterns. That way, you can emphasize your good behaviors and be aware of others that have tripped you up in the past.

Manage Your Ongoing Behavior and Follow-Through: You will learn how to make good "bad" financial decisions. Using our method, you will be able to determine when a decision that might not be good for others is really good for you and the life you want to live. Sometimes, it feels great to make a "bad" financial decision when you are doing it intentionally. I will show you how.

When Things Don't Go as Planned, and They Won't

A good Life Plan is a living, breathing thing. As your needs and circumstances change, you must modify your plan accordingly.

Life-Builders

Answer the following questions in your journal or notebook to gain a better understanding of your big-picture vision for your life.

1. What do you worry about?

2. What things in life would you really like to plan for? List as many as you can without worrying how that planning will happen.

3. What would it feel like to have a realistic plan for these items and experiences? Be specific.

4. What is keeping you from planning for these things? Be as detailed and honest with yourself as possible.

Know Yourself

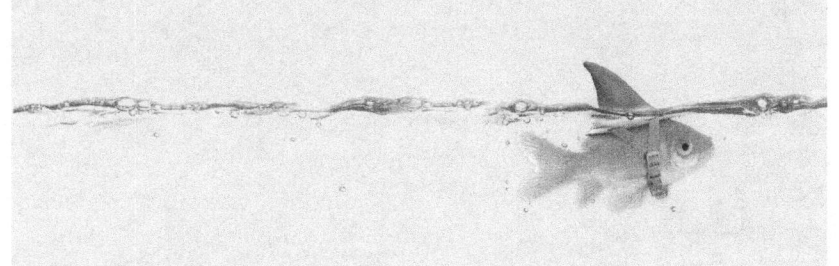

CHAPTER 4

UN-SURPRISE
YOUR TENDENCIES

"The main thing is to keep the main thing the main thing."
— *Stephen Covey*

Pick the statement below that you identify with the most. Don't overthink it.

A. More is better. The best way to a great life is to pack in as much as possible in terms of life experiences, relationships, and purchases. I am in awe of the amazing opportunities that exist in the world, and I want to enjoy as many as possible. Sometimes I take risks with the future because nothing is promised.

OR

B. Less and later are better. As part of my great life, I value security and steadiness. I am selective. I like to "win by not losing." Also, I am making sacrifices now in the name of something bigger later.

We all have beliefs about spending money and, whether we realize it or not, a formula for living. In my work, I've noticed patterns and tendencies among people in their approaches to spending. There are two different approaches that identify the type of consumer you are, and between them, apply to virtually everyone.

There are the "more" people and the "wait for something later" people.

Let's define these two approaches further. I have developed names for each of them.

More Is Better: The Maxers

Some people feel that the best way to a great life is to keep piling more on in terms of experiences and purchases. They want the max(imum) experience of everything possible. I like to call this group the Maxers. You are likely to see them driving luxury cars, living in large houses, and taking fancy vacations. They live more heavily in the present and also value material things and "wow" experiences more.

Later Is Better: The Waiters

Waiters seek safety and value frugality. They often delay gratification in the name of something later. A Waiter may take pride in their frugality and perceived ability to weather a variety of storms and have things work out in the end. If overdone, though, a mindless waiting approach can also be dangerous.

A Little Bit of Both?

You may find that you exhibit qualities of both great life approaches in different facets of your life. Keep up your awareness of that, and see what you can learn from it.

Neither the "more" nor the "waiting" approach is wrong.

A Waiter might think that a Maxer is misguided for being such a rabid consumer. Meanwhile, the Maxer could think that the Waiter is just waiting pointlessly, and that it's no way to live life. But neither of these approaches is wrong *if done mindfully and with intention*.

I'm not here to judge the lens you use to view the life you want to live. You have a lot of history and experience that I may never be able to fully understand. My wish is that you will be authentic in who you are and how you approach your life. I've seen both Maxers and Waiters live wonderful lives.

The out-of-control Maxer story is the one we hear the most, and I've seen it firsthand. They are the people who overindulge and get into heavy credit-card debt or even declare bankruptcy because they overextended themselves with lavish life experiences. But the Waiter who mindlessly waits can be just as dangerous to themselves. I've seen far too many missed opportunities by Waiters who fail to take advantage of opportunities that could benefit them. Too many have regrets when it's too late to enjoy their savings because of health challenges or because they no longer have someone to enjoy spending it with.

Very different routes to an unhappy ending. So what is the solution?

Regardless of which camp you fall into, the key is to do it *intentionally*. If you are going to be a Maxer, be a *mindful Maxer*; if you are going to be a Waiter, be a *mindful Waiter*.

In either case of regrets, they made their decisions without intentionality. If you're going to wait, be specific about it. If you are going to pile on more things, understand what is meaningful enough for you now that you might be willing to sacrifice later in the name of that thing.

As evidenced by my next story, which went viral on the internet, unintended outcomes can be very sneaky if you are not crystal clear about what you want to achieve.

Giving Unintentionality a Bad Name

In 2016, the National Environment Research Council (NERC) of the British government set forth to name a $287 million polar research ship that would soon be christened. It was a beautiful, state-of-the-art vessel, and they wanted an appropriate name. The NERC decided to ask the public to vote, and the winning name would be the official name of this vessel.

They suggested what they felt were dignified names like Shackleton, Endeavor, and Falcon, but it was up to the public to pick names and vote. If you guessed that the mischievous public on the internet would be up to their old tricks, you were right. After weeks of voting, there was a clear winning name by a landslide, and it was...
Boaty McBoatface.

The second-place name was Poppy-Mai, which was the name of a young girl with cancer whose story had captured the hearts of many.

Poppy-Mai received 34,371 votes. McBoatface won by a staggering margin with 121,109 votes.

The NERC didn't apply one of Stephen Covey's rules, which was to "keep the main thing the main thing."

Sure, the idea of having a public naming contest was cute, but…

- It was not consistent with their main outcome of doing cutting-edge environmental research.

- They are researchers, not marketers, and they weren't prepared to consider the potential ramifications of holding a naming contest.

By not being crystal clear about the end result, the NERC made a huge mistake. Now, they had a public relations nightmare on their hands. The internet was ticked off.

After a long, drawn-out process, the NERC had a plan for moving forward with a name. I can only imagine how much this took in terms of time and resources—time and resources not directed at their main outcome of environmental research. The ship was eventually named *Sir David Attenborough*, but a small submersible on the ship was named *Boaty McBoatface* as a consolation.

As Lewis Carroll said, "If you don't know where you are going, any road will get you there." So take time to find what is most important for you.

It's easy to see how they were distracted. The same can apply to us. Things can pop up in life that can send us off course. Whether it's a perceived threat in the eyes of a more frugal person or a seemingly "great opportunity" in the eyes of someone who is more aggressive in their life approach. The antidote for this is to define your life goals clearly and tie any of your decisions to them. Commit to being intentional.

Mindful Maxers

To be clear, becoming a mindful Maxer does not mean you need to temper your excitable nature or stop being a dreamer. It just requires some time up front to think about what "more" actually gives you and how it could effectively give you less in terms of what you want in the big picture.

Full disclosure: I am a Maxer. I understand and accept this tendency, and I wouldn't change it. However, as you'll see in my planning approach outlined in this book, I have a mindful awareness of this tendency and use it to my advantage.

Mindful Maxers: An Example

Let's talk more about the value of intentionality and how it helps you draw conclusions you may not arrive at otherwise.

We know a husband and wife, who we'll call Bob and Sandy. She is 58 and he is 81. Unfortunately, Sandy is dealing with glaucoma, which is worsening and likely to take most, if not all, of her eyesight within a relatively short period of time. These two are adventurers, so much so that Bob was behind the development of a major trail system here in the US. They have significant assets, but not so much that they can do whatever they want whenever they want. They have a long list of experiences they want to share—now rather than later, for obvious reasons. Should they just go for it?

There are all kinds of risks. Long-term care is a possibility for him, and it's an even stronger possibility for her down the road.

With all that in mind, we crunched their numbers and agreed the answer for them was actually "Yes, let's do it!" Might sound reckless, but it's quite the opposite. It is highly calculated. They came up with the term "front-loading the fun" to describe what they were doing.

Could there be risks later? Yes.

Are there certain contingencies where they might be left slightly more exposed? Yes.

Are they doing it anyway? Yes, they're mindful Maxers.

You see, the difference here is that they're being honest with themselves, looking at the numbers, and going forth anyway. That's my wish for you. This couple had the choice to not do detailed planning and hope things worked out, in the way many people handle traditional retirement planning—just save their money for later. Or they could put their heads in the sand and go on all of these trips. But can you see how that would cause significant uneasiness for them? In this case, they are moving forward intentionally and with confidence.

So just to summarize this concept of intentionality, there's an excellent quote by the late, great Charlie Munger, who was Warren Buffett's business partner for many years.

> *"It is remarkable how much long-term advantage people like us have gotten by trying to be consistently not stupid, instead of trying to be very intelligent."*

By being intentional, you will avoid those not-so-smart pitfalls and make the moves that are smart for you.

The Mindful Waiter

To be a mindful Waiter, it's all about defining what you are waiting for and what reasonable risks you are protecting against.

- **Define the reasonable risks and costs associated with them.** It may be a good idea to reasonably overstate them. A common approach is to add spending when running projections, even though money is not likely to be spent. In doing so, if your financial plan projections still work out, this may provide a little more confidence.

- **Define the endpoint.** What are some things you would do if you knew everything would work out?

- **Identify the cost of inaction in detail.** Later when you learn about making data-driven decisions, you'll realize how critical it is to identify the cost of inaction around the spending you avoid or delay.

- **Dip your toe in.** Once you have identified some possible life experience targets in the cost of inaction, give it a little try in a controlled environment.

- **Celebrate.** Making some additional mindful consumption choices will likely still feel uncomfortable for quite a while. With that in mind, be sure to celebrate when you make an intentional choice to have an experience that you would have otherwise avoided or postponed. This is a big deal, and it will help guide you toward a more balanced approach.

What Do Maxers and Waiters Have in Common?

You may notice that in various facets of life, you exhibit qualities of both Maxers and Waiters. That's totally understandable, because there is something specific behind both of these behaviors.

It's our relationship with fear.

The Maxer fears that not packing in enough good will cause them to miss out, and the Waiter fears that not being prepared for potential bad things will derail them.

Spend time identifying your fears around long-term planning. Identify which worries are rational and which ones are irrational. Choosing to make data-driven decisions over emotional ones is a good place to start on this, and this is one of my favorite ways we help our clients find clarity and confidence in their plans.

The best approach for data-driven decisions is to work backward. In your financial planning, identify how much of a cushion you want to have at the end of life, and consider various scenarios based on that assumption.

How Do You Feel About Leftovers?

By leftovers, I mean leaving money behind after you die. Your death is (hopefully) a long way off in the future, but it offers a simple place to start with intentionality.

For some people, an interesting place to start is to decide whether they want to have money left over at the end of life or not. I find that our clients are broken into two main groups:

A. "If we have money left over, we would like to leave it to the kids."

B. "We contributed a lot to the kids by raising and educating them, and we are going to enjoy the money we have as much as we can. In a perfect world, we would spend it all and die with very little money left over."

You can start your intentionality journey by picking one of these approaches. Later, the next step might be to identify exactly how much you would want your kids or other loved ones to inherit. This way, you can avoid the ambiguity of wealth transfer to your kids. Too many people miss opportunities because they wish to leave money to their kids but are unclear on the amount. As a result, they sometimes miss experiences because they are saving most or all of their discretionary income for their kids, when perhaps they don't need to.

Let's say you have two kids and want to leave each of them $500,000 at the end of your life. Setting these types of intentions will increase your confidence as you evaluate life's opportunities that come your way.

What Is Intentional Inefficiency?

When you are really dialed in with your intentionality, you can start to have some fun with it.

One of the reasons I work hard is for the luxury of an occasional "sloppy" purchase. I recall sitting at a dinner with friends at a nice restaurant when I was in my early twenties. A friend who had already hit it big in technology picked up the tab for all of us. I thought, *I want to be able to do that!* I have smart money habits with the important things, but I wanted the ability to occasionally make purchases that weren't "smart."

That was the beginning of my "intentional inefficiency." Every once in a while, I love to pick up the tab for dinner or buy an overpriced T-shirt at a sporting event. I can do this without judging myself for it because I have a general idea of how much I can spend without taking money from the future goals that Lindsay and I have intentionally determined for ourselves. Plus, being frivolous on purpose is a fun reward for our hard work.

It feels great to have a well-constructed Life Plan that considers many different variables so you can give yourself some room to make smart splurges.

Finding an Intentional Track

Remember the "How do I know if I'm on track?" question from earlier? Hopefully, you are starting to see by now why this is an incomplete question and how to instead live on purpose.

The message in this chapter is to dig into your default settings and pair that with the concept of intentionality, so you can be a more refined version of yourself. With this increased awareness, you can be more comfortable in your daily decisions knowing that you will be more selective based on your big-picture desired outcome.

Commit now to be more intentional in your decisions. In the next chapter, I will provide you with something that is even bigger than your goals to help guide your decisions and life experience.

Life-Builders

1. What are some scenarios where you are intentionally financially inefficient and you love it? Be sure to celebrate these and show gratitude for the hard work you do to make this possible.

2. What other behavior patterns or tendencies can you uncover that will give you clues for better decision-making in the future?

CHAPTER 5

FIND YOUR FINGERPRINTS

*"Values are like fingerprints.
Nobody's are the same, but you leave them all over
everything you do."*

— *often attributed to Elvis Presley*

Your values are the *reasons* for your goals. They are the anchor for when your life hits a bumpy patch *or* when opportunity knocks. Can you rattle off your top five personal values in life right now? You should be able to.

Goal-setting is great, and kudos to you if you are doing that already. But aligning your financial planning with your values is even better. Think of them as your "me" words—the five beliefs that describe your mission in life. If you don't have a clear idea of these values, you may have a hard time with intentionality.

We do a really cool values identification exercise with clients. I learned this exercise in the Behavioral Financial Advisor Certificate program. Here's how it works. Grab a bowl of ice cream or a glass of wine. (You already like this more than crunching financial numbers, don't you?) If you have a partner or spouse, do this exercise separately and then share your values with each other afterward. Even doing this exercise can be a profound experience and spur great conversations.

Finding Your Fingerprints

The values exercise can be found on our website at www. WheelerFinancial-llc.com/values_exercise. If you are on your computer, you can do it right now.

On the landing page, you will see a deck of 50 cards, each with something you may value on it. Possible values on each of the cards are things like...

- Adventure
- Faith
- Family
- Money
- Power
- Relationships
- Status

To complete the exercise, you start discarding the cards with values that are not meaningful and move any of the values that could be a candidate to be one of your core values. Gradually, you will narrow these 50 cards down until you get to 15. Then you narrow those 15 down to 5. You have then identified your five most important values.

Then you ask yourself this big question:

Is the life I am living in alignment with my most important values?

If your answer is yes, that's great. But it's also okay if the answer is no. At least you know now, right? Then you can review and adjust your Life Plan accordingly.

Knowing your values is a major step in creating a new "How do I know if I'm on track?" question.

Is the life I am living in alignment with my most important values?

"On track" is no longer just about your income and accounts, like the fact that your 401(k) balance is trending upward so you'll likely be able to fund your retirement sufficiently.

With your values identified, you can answer whether you are on track with living out the purpose you have created for your life.

Values in Your Daily Life

The beauty of these values is that they now serve as a guide for any opportunities or challenges that come your way. You'd be amazed at how much more confident you can be in your decision-making when you can tie it back to clearly defined values.

I am reminded of a story about a gentleman who was facing a difficult health situation. He had cancer and was going through treatment. The prognosis was not good. At the same time, something came up in his professional life where he felt like he had been severely wronged. It was a difficult situation. He contacted an attorney and was pursuing a lawsuit.

I decided it was time to do the values exercise with him.

He had done the values exercise at home, and we later discussed the results. I could tell he was struggling and that the treatment was taking a toll on him.

Three of the values he identified were harmony, adventure, and relationships.

I asked, "Is pursuing a lawsuit for money you don't actually need in alignment with your values?"

The clarity was immediate—so much so that on the way home from my office, he called his attorney and requested that they settle the matter quickly for whatever they could get. For him, time was more important than money. His values served as a strong foundation during tough times.

I'm pleased to say that this person made a recovery and has gone on to have some awesome experiences in keeping with his values.

You will be amazed at the clarity and confidence you get simply by taking the time to explore your values and using them as a guide.

What Do Values-Based Goals Look Like?

Let's start to tie this together. In the previous chapter, you committed to intentionality. By adding a focus on your values, you are building on that. Those lead to super goal creation.

Let's say you have a daughter who is 15 and really wants the family to go on an expensive hiking tour of Europe before she goes to college. Also imagine that her 529 plan (a type of college savings account) funding is below where you would like it to be.

If your top five values include family, adventure, and profound experiences, this might guide you to take the trip even if it means she could have some college debt.

But what if your five values included education, security, and frugality? In that case, you may decide that your mission is to give her a solid financial and educational foundation, and if she wants to take that trip later once she's established, she can.

Your values are the reasons for your goals, and they help you to discern whether the opportunity is good for you.

Values-Based Relationship Goals

Are you treating the people you care about in alignment with your values?

Are any of your relationships out of alignment with your values?

This could be worth some thought and analysis on your part.

As it pertains to relationships, knowing your values can be useful when tensions run high. You may be able to create a more thoughtful response under pressure.

Value clarity also work wonders for couples. Knowing your partner's values can help you understand why you agree—or disagree—on major Life Planning decisions. I am not a couples therapist, and I'm not qualified to give relationship advice. I will say, though, that the couples I've worked with who know and respect each other's values tend to be in a much better position for strong financial decision-making.

Values-Based Big-Ticket Purchases

There you are in the car dealership showroom. It's a real beauty... an absolutely gorgeous vehicle.

And also way over your budget.

But your heart is pumping with the exhilaration of making this amazing car yours. Your inner salesperson is putting on the hard close even more than your actual salesperson is.

Could it be the right vehicle for you? It might be.

Check in with your values. Is it still "the one"?

I'm not suggesting that you deprive yourself of everything. Quite the opposite, in fact. I just want you to deprive yourself of things that aren't meaningful to you. Recalling your values in the heat of the moment is good for that.

Values-Based Work Goals

I love my job. As you can probably imagine, the personal satisfaction derived from helping people make major life-shifting decisions is tremendously rewarding. It can also be stressful helping people through difficult situations, managing their investments through volatility in the stock market, and coaching them as account balances rise and fall.

Because *family* and *relationships* are included in my personal values, I use those to check myself regarding how much I'm taking on at work and how my job is affecting those areas. I'm not perfect with it, but I think about this balance every single day.

While it may seem counterintuitive, I believe that not making work "the main thing" makes me a better and more relatable advisor. And it goes without saying that it makes me a better husband and dad.

Your Values May Evolve

I also like to check in with my values each year. Life circumstances tend to change, and my values evolve. I reflect on them each year in December. Some years, I also repeat the values exercise.

Set aside time every year to review yours as well, as they often serve as the cornerstone for your decision-making. However, be careful of the temptation to adjust your values in the midst of a major decision. You could be tricking yourself.

Once you have un-surprised your values and the way they can affect your decisions, you have built a solid foundation for your planning. Your next step will be to build on this by identifying the many surprising things in life that could otherwise catch you off guard. This can include your possessions, your health, and even relationships with the people you care most about. With values-based decisions and clarity around the previously unexpected, you will continue to pave your way to increased clarity and confidence in your planning.

Life-Builders

Answer the questions below in a journal or notebook to get more clarity on whether you are living a life in alignment with your values.

1. What is one thing in your life that is the *most* in alignment with your values right now? What can you learn from that?

2. What is one thing in your life that is the *least* in alignment with your values right now? What can you learn from that?

3. What is one thing you might change to help your life become more aligned with your values?

4. Who is one person in your life whose values you would like to learn more about? I suggest you recommend our values identification exercise to them and discuss the results.

Guide Yourself

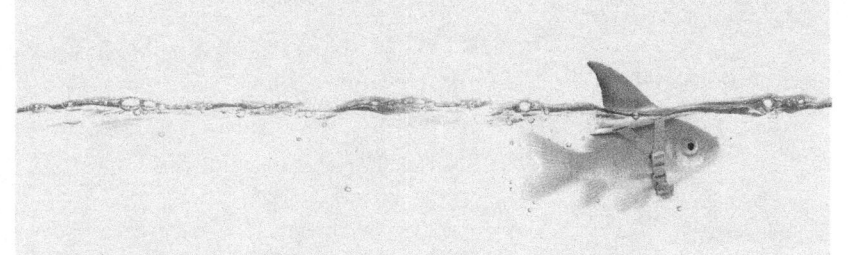

CHAPTER 6

PREPARE FOR THE PREDICTABLE

"The time to repair the roof is when the sun is shining."

— *John F. Kennedy,*
1962 State of the Union Address

There is a lot to learn about the life you want to live, but you can start by taking notice of all the predictable things that are likely to happen. You might believe these things are totally out of your control, but you can do a better job of paying attention now so they don't catch you off guard in the future.

Once you learn this approach, you will be amazed at how many things in life have been surprising you...that should not be surprising at all.

The areas of your life where you can "un-surprise yourself" include your house, your cars, your time with the people you care most about, and even your own reaction patterns. This method even helps you lessen some of the discomfort from *real surprises* that can come your way.

On Thanksgiving morning in 2012, I was excited to wake up early because the holiday afforded me some much-needed time to work on a special gift for our son and daughter. I was restoring the train set my Pop Pop had made when I was a kid, and I hoped to finish by Christmas.

As I walked down the carpeted stairs to the basement, my last step was a wet *squish*. I discovered that the bottom of my 80-gallon water heater had rusted out and released its contents all over the floor of my finished basement. I was surprised—but I shouldn't have been. Truth is, I was gambling with the life of my 17-year-old water heater. It just so happens that I lost the bet that day.

This happens to many of us around the management of our homes. We often delay home repairs for one of three reasons:

- We prioritize something else more fun because potential issues are currently not causing us any pain.

- We are trying to be thrifty and squeeze the last ounce of life out of the item.

- Our lives are busy, and we either didn't think about it or put it off.

But there is good news! Most home repairs are completely unsurprising. Every item in your home has a relatively predictable life expectancy.

Un-Surprising Your House

Here's how you can un-surprise your house. Start by listing all the components inside it. For example, you have an HVAC system, roof, windows, doors…a kitchen and bathrooms you may want to upgrade or replace…a hot water heater, carpet, paint, etc. Next, determine when each item was last replaced, or use a reliable estimate.

Now, add the average life expectancy for each one. Let's say you need to replace your water heater every 12 years. If it was last replaced in 2019, you will need a new water heater in 2031. Finally, add the (current) average cost of replacement for each item.

Now you have a list of all the years you will need to replace various systems in your house, and you have a general idea of how much they will cost. That way, if you decide to splurge on a huge Hawaiian vacation and your old roof starts to leak, you won't be caught off guard. It's really not that surprising with some good preparation.

Take a look below at our home maintenance schedule. I encourage you to complete this list for your own house within the next 14 days. It doesn't matter whether you know the exact dates of last replacement yet. Do the best you can now, and clean up the details later.

Wheeler Financial's Home Maintenance Schedule

Project	Last Done	Life Span	Replace In	Estimated Cost
HVAC		15		$16,000
Roof		20		$18,000
Windows		30		$18,000
Entry Doors		30		$4,000
Kitchen		25		$60,000
Master Bath		25		$18,000
Main Bath		25		$18,000
Powder Room		25		$7,500
Garage Door		30		$4,000
Paint		7		$6,000
Water Heater		12		$1,500
Washer/Dryer		12		$2,000
Tree Work		10		$3,500
Carpets		15		$4,000
Hardwoods		20		$6,000
Driveway		30		$12,000
Sump Pumps		15		$1,200
Landscaping		10		$5,000
Patio/Deck		25		$20,000
Siding		35		$15,000

Un-surprising your house…check!

Un-Surprising Your Time and Much More

My good friend Keith and I were out on the golf course a while back on a beautiful summer day, talking about life and age. (I was 46 at the time.)

He said, "We're on the back nine, buddy." He was referring to our game of life, not golf.

It really shook me up. I became concerned about the time I had left with everyone I cared about. We only had a few years until the kids went off to college. It was a turning point in my life.

It still sticks in my head. As much as I feel so fortunate to have a wonderful wife, kids, family, friends, house, business, and coworkers…time keeps on ticking.

An occasional and intentional check-in with the scarcity of time can be truly impactful. To check in with our own mortality is to turn off the autopilot for a bit and "un-surprise" the urgency that exists around planning for and living the life we dream of.

But you're only doing it right if you also acknowledge the abundance of great things in your life. Merging the abundance of life as it exists now with the opportunity that exists before us can be powerful.

Once you've acknowledged the scarcity of time and committed to taking an abundant, intentional approach, it's time to organize what's possible for you and your remaining lifetime. I encourage you to start by reflecting on these questions:

1. What are the top 20 vacations you'd like to go on?

2. What are some important goals you'd like to accomplish with your kids? With your parents?

3. What are some "toys" you'd like to have? New cars? A boat?

4. What goals do you have around work and career?

5. Did you always want to learn the guitar? You can add that to your map.

The act of imagining what you might want to do in life and then seeing the limited amount of time and money to fit it all in provides an eye-opening perspective.

Un-Surprising the Time You Have with Loved Ones

The people in our lives aren't going to be around forever, and it's important to be honest with ourselves about that. I encourage you to write down the ages of the people you care about most as well as likely milestones in their life. And by including their life expectancy, you can see the urgency right there on the page.

Make sure you have those critical conversations while you can. You may also find that the scarcity of time you have with parents or kids living at home influences how you manage your money.

Lean into it, and don't be surprised.

Un-Surprising Your Life Experiences

Let's say you are a big traveler, and there are 15 places in the world you are just dying to see. You determine that you can afford to go on a big trip every other year. This means it will take you *30 years* to complete all this traveling! Map them out, prioritize them, and see what you can realistically do.

The magic starts to happen as you plan around your realistic picture of the future. For example, is it a good idea to plan the trip for Hawaii during the same year you want to do your kitchen, your oldest starts college, and you want to buy a car for your child who is turning 16? Probably not. So a clear plan in advance for these experiences can dramatically increase the probability of them happening.

Un-Surprising Your Health

Our health is going to make some of life's decisions for us. For example, I love running. It's one of my favorite things to do. In fact, if I'm being a grouch after work, Lindsay might tell me to go out for a run, because she knows I will come back 30 minutes later much nicer and more relaxed. My Saturday trail runs with friends are a social highlight of my week. We run four or five miles, have some good laughs, and solve all the world's problems.

Unfortunately, I have a bad back, so I'm not always going to be able to run like that. Knowing that helps me appreciate it now so much more. I'm also aware of how it will affect my choices and my money. If there is an expensive treatment that would keep me running for longer, I would certainly consider that. I may not like having to pay for it, but if I've planned ahead, at least I won't be surprised by it.

If I do have to discontinue running, I have other activities planned to replace that.

You may look at your life and think about your likelihood of being alive and healthy at your kids' weddings or for the birth of your grandchildren. This may inspire you to take better care of your body.

There are tools such as biological age calculators to determine how your choices may affect the way you age. But chances are, you know whether you need to make changes. An important step is to get annual checkups and follow up on any health concerns to ensure you remain in the best shape for as long as possible.

I have seen too many well-funded retirements not go as planned due to health challenges or premature death. Use the reality of the experiences you may miss to influence your health decisions.

Un-Surprising Your Behavioral Patterns

Un-surprising your reactions to things can benefit your relationships and overall life experience. It's important to identify your common behavioral patterns. One way to learn about these tendencies is to ask the people you care about to give a candid assessment of what they observe about your behaviors.

Try this: Identify someone who knows you really well and spends a lot of time with you. It could be a spouse, best friend, or your child (teenage or older). Then ask them these questions.

- Which of my behavior patterns do you think serve me the best? Which of my habits would you most want to adopt yourself?

- Which patterns or tendencies do you think challenge me the most?

- What is something I do often that I might not be aware of?

It's like watching a film about your life. Jim Nelson, who works in our practice, had an eight-year career as a linebacker in the NFL and knows the value of watching film.

If you saw in your "game film" that your typical reaction to a bad day at work was to drink three glasses of red wine—which then leads to mindless scrolling, and next thing you know, you are on the Amazon app...and a couple days later, three boxes show up on your front step—maybe there is something you can learn from that.

Get curious about those behavior patterns, and see how you can notice them in everyday life.

Actual Surprises

You can get ahead of a fair number of actual surprises, too.

On a Tuesday in November 2020, I took my five-year-old sedan to the auto repair center for a routine service. The car had 53,000 miles on it. The mechanic called with bad news: a code in the diagnostics indicated that a catastrophic engine issue could be coming. He suggested that I get rid of the car as soon as possible.

Wow—I was not expecting that. I loved that car and had planned to hold on to it for five more years. Now I needed to go buy a new one...quickly.

Two days later, we and the kids took Lindsay's SUV to get COVID tests, which were being administered at a local minor league baseball stadium. Just as we exited the stadium parking lot, I noticed what looked like steam coming from under the hood. I looked at the dashboard gauges and everything seemed fine.

But I decided to pull over, and I told everyone to get out of the car immediately. As we stepped back, Lindsay pointed out flames coming from underneath the car. Within what felt like 10 seconds, the car was fully engulfed in fire. Thankfully, the Wilmington Fire Department arrived in a hurry, and they quickly extinguished it.

Aside from the effects of seeing our car catch fire and hearing the tires explode, we were all fine. We escaped without physical injury. But of course her car was not okay. It was only seven years old, had 76,000 miles on it, and I thought it had been in perfect condition. It clearly wasn't.

Now we needed two cars.

Were we surprised? Hell yeah—that was a real surprise!

Were we surprised financially? Hell no.

Lindsay and I had a CARS account where we had been setting aside a certain amount of money each month to prepare for our next car purchase. Our choice to save that money instead of using it on something else paid big dividends for us in that instance. It was a surprising event for sure, but it didn't catch us completely off guard. Within the next two weeks, we picked up two new cars. It wasn't exactly the way we had planned things, but life seldom is.

Un-Surprising Your Family Care

All too frequently, we see families who are caught off guard by unexpected health issues with their aging parents. There are ways to be organized for this. Start with the following suggested care plan for your parents and work with any family members to share their responsibilities associated with your parents' care. Here is a handy summary of some possible roles to fill.

Parent Support Roles

GENERAL

- **Transportation Manager:** Provide transportation and/ or make arrangements for people to drive parent(s) when needed.

- **Housing Coordinator/Home Improvement Liaison:** Ensure the home is in safe and working order, and coordinate with contractors as needed. If a parent needs long-term care, oversee the research and selection discussion with the family.

- **Food Coordinator:** Manage nutrition needs and buy groceries.

- **Communication Liaison:** Ensure that all family members are up-to-date on important information regarding parents.

- **Primary Caregiver:** This person is the primary day-to-day care manager. Some duties may be delegated, but this person is generally in charge of basic activities at the house.

- **Emotional Support:** Offer emotional support to parents and siblings.

- **Financial Affairs Manager:** Handle all areas of finances including paying bills, managing investments, and obtaining long-term care insurance (if applicable).

- **Estate Planning Coordinator:** Keep all legal documents in order and make arrangements to have them updated as necessary.

HEALTH

- **Medical Appointment Coordinator:** Schedule all medical appointments and related follow-up care.

- **Medication Coordinator:** Ensure that prescriptions are filled as necessary.

Un-Surprising Results

I hope you can now understand why I view a financial plan as a puzzle. There are so many pieces we can find if we look for them. Some are easier than others. Start with the achievable part by identifying the potential surprises that are easy for you to spot. This is like sorting out the edge pieces.

Becoming aware of your "surprises" will have a profound effect on your money decisions. It could mean prioritizing that vacation with your parents or that trip to Disney with your kids before they get too old for it. It could mean taking better care of yourself. It could be just a meaningful reflection on the scarcity and fragility of our time on Earth.

Please don't skip this act of scanning your life for both predictable and unpredictable future expenses. Hopefully, you've learned that an important part of planning is simply the act of…

- Identifying all the things you could be surprised by.

- Recrafting your reaction to them.

As you continue to read, you will learn more about the value of not leading with the money part.

Life-Builders

Answer the following questions to discover which actions are needed around your money, your health, your relationships, and more.

1. What is a conversation or experience you commit to having with a person with whom you have limited time to spend together? Examples could include:

   a. Taking a special vacation with your high school junior whose time living at home may be limited

   b. Asking an older loved one questions to learn more about their life experience while you can

   c. Checking off a "bucket list" item, alone or with someone else

2. What difficult conversation would you like to have with someone? How would you feel if you lost the opportunity to have that talk because they were no longer in your life? Consider actions you can take to improve this relationship while you still can.

3. What is the first area of your life you would like to "un-surprise"? What is the first step you will take?

CHAPTER 7

SIX SAVVY RULES FOR IMPACTFUL PLANNING

"Not everything that can be counted counts, and not everything that counts can be counted."

— *William Bruce Cameron*

Many of us think that to be "on track" with a great financial plan, we need to be a math whiz and track every penny, monitoring our budgets, accounts, investments, and other financial data on a daily basis. This is one reason for getting off track, in my opinion, because many common strategies for measuring whether you are on track simply aren't fun. If it's not fun, you're probably not going to be excited about it, right?

These six rules are my personal hacks for simplifying your planning and, dare I say, making it more fun!

Rule #1: Remember that in the absence of data, your emotions take over your decision-making.

Emotions are really useful in the *right* parts of the decision-making process...but they can be a hindrance in other parts.

How can you tell the difference?

I often see clients get carried away with emotion when making decisions. The result tends to be that they overemphasize the short-term without considering certain long-term consequences. Whenever you can, try to find data points to help make a more objective decision.

I'm totally fine with using a gut feeling as a tiebreaker; however, it can be dangerous to lead with your gut. I've dedicated the rest of this chapter to help you easily expose some valuable data points in everyday life.

Put a number behind it when you can. Data is also an important part of the answer to "Am I on track?" You need to have some things to measure to tell whether you are headed in the right direction.

Rule #2: Know how much that feeling costs.

What feeling are you buying?

How much does it cost?

Is it worth it?

Jacques and Elise were introduced to me in 2017 by their daughter, Judy. They were amazing human beings right up until they passed away in their eighties and nineties.

They were also big-time Waiters.

Jacques and Elise were indeed very frugal. Jacques worked for KLM Airlines in many roles, including being a steward during the glory days of commercial flight. While he was never a huge earner, they were cautious with their money as he and Elise, a dedicated homemaker, raised their five children.

As a result of their frugality, they built up a significant savings. When we first met, a large portion of their investments was extremely conservative, which didn't surprise me. We uncovered that their house needed major maintenance, they were driving a car that was way too old, and they could really use some help around the house as they were aging. Examples such as this are relatively common for Waiters as they age.

Jacques and Elise had built up over $250,000 in checking and savings accounts, which they had held at this level for over 25 years, even though the interest rate on cash had been quite low for some time. When I see this, I approach it with curiosity.

I asked, "What feeling does it give you to have this large amount of cash?"

"Security and safety in case of an emergency," Jacques said.

Over time, I would find out that Jacques and Elise had both been orphaned during the Holocaust and had experienced unspeakable tragedy and hardship in their youth. They were making emotional money decisions for good reason. However, these emotional decisions were affecting their quality of life, and their adult children were concerned about them. It became clear that it would be helpful to add some data to the emotions and experience driving their decisions.

I responded, "That is totally understandable. Tell me what specific emergencies you are planning for."

Jacques and Elise didn't have an answer here, and that's not uncommon.

I said, "No problem. In the past twenty-five years or so, have you used this emergency fund for anything?"

Elise said, "No, it never really occurred to us. We were able to get by without it so far."

"How much do you think that feeling of safety and security has cost you over the years?"

"I never really thought of it that way," she said.

Many people don't think of it this way. Remember, you can only invest each dollar in one place, so you need to be very thoughtful.

We agreed that I would think about their situation, and we would meet again to discuss my thoughts. I knew that if I could help them understand the cost of the feelings they were "buying" with their conservative cash accounts, they would be able to apply this to their other money.

I suggested they take their low-yielding, conservative cash account and compare it to a moderately conservative allocation, while still leaving approximately $100,000 in cash for emergencies. We will call that Allocation B. When comparing their cash account to Allocation B, we estimated that this account could have potentially outperformed their cash by about $132,000 over that time. They now knew the cost of that feeling.

I asked Elise, "Is that feeling of security worth approximately $132,000 to you?"

"No. Definitely not!"

There was still a lot of work for them to be done, but at that moment they decided to use the data to help them take a step back from powerful emotions around money. This is another example of how mindful Waiters are made.

I taught them how to put a number on the emergency fund they would realistically need by looking at possible negative situations and the probability of them happening.

Eventually, they were able to use a more specific methodology to determine the amount they kept in an emergency fund and knew exactly what it was for.

After careful consideration, they spent some of their cash account to improve their house, and they got a caretaker to help them as they both faced significant health challenges. Elise bought herself a nice new car so she could drive herself to play the recorder with friends, which she did right up until her passing at age 92 in 2023.

More on the Cost of a Feeling

If you think about it, money is just a means of exchange for a feeling. And if you think back to the hedonic thermostat, you'll recall these feelings are often fleeting. One way to determine the cost of these feelings is to be honest with yourself. We can be quite good at tricking ourselves and justifying things.

Your financial decisions could be associated with some of these feelings:

- Control
- Envy
- Freedom
- Gratitude
- Guilt
- Happiness
- Outward Perception of Success
- Peace
- Pride
- Security

When you are buying something or saving money for a specific purpose, seek awareness of the feelings behind it. You should be able to answer these questions:

- How much of that feeling will this purchase actually give me?
- How much will it cost?
- Is it worth it in the context of other things I want to do in my life?

Rule #3: Use your financial numbers to make key decisions.

Much of the work leading up to this point can be done on your own. In some instances, it can be amplified or accelerated with the help of an experienced professional, but it's still a lot of personal work identifying your values, thinking about this great life you want to live, and being intentional about it.

Regardless of whether you do this planning on your own or with support, you must know the numbers behind the decisions you make and the likely financial results behind them.

Good financial management is just a big game of trade-offs.

When we start with new clients, we hold what we call a "messy meeting." The beauty of this meeting is that we let it be messy by design. We take their life as it stands right now, and we model a bunch of different scenarios using sophisticated financial planning software. Anything they can think of—the trip to Disney…cars for the kids at age 16… early retirement…paying 100% of college tuition. We throw in all those scenarios and mix and match them until we find a plan that works. It's a great way of showing clients the effects of different decisions they make, and it trains them to use their data for making decisions.

This is why we don't discount the value of emotion in the decision-making process. This meeting is typically very emotional, but when we put numbers behind it, a certain degree of rationality starts to emerge. It's fun to be a part of it.

Good financial management is just a big game of trade-offs.

My wife Lindsay and I really want a vacation home at the Delaware beaches, and the one we want won't be cheap. We've talked about it for years. It's so important to us that we use it to help us make other decisions.

We realize that every financial decision—the splurges and the necessary—we make now will impact when we finally close on that beach house. With every dollar spent, we are trading time there later for something else now.

When an opportunity pops up, we ask ourselves, "Is it worth delaying the beach house?"

Think of something big that you really want and use that to evaluate every financial decision. Your meaningful item could be a vacation home, or it could be leaving a job that is wearing you down.

You are essentially making trade-offs but know *exactly* what you are trading. This further illustrates the importance of knowing your numbers.

Beware of Traps

If you're going to do your own financial planning, beware of the Dunning-Kruger effect. That's when people with limited competence in a particular area overestimate their abilities.

I'm not suggesting you can't do it yourself. It can absolutely be done. But don't underestimate the amount of time needed to become highly knowledgeable in this area. I've seen many people move forward with a plan who did not understand its effects in a big-picture context.

Sure, there are a lot of financial ideas available at your fingertips these days, and they can be useful. Just as you would have a vetting process for choosing a financial advisor, you should also verify any ideas you find on the internet.

You may identify important numbers such as net cash flow, debt ratio, or savings rate, but knowing specific numbers is not the point; using those numbers to make solid decisions is the point. When clients delegate their financial planning to us, I sometimes joke that the only number they need to know is our phone number. I just want them to know the concept of making financial decisions using their important numbers, and we help them do that.

Rule #4: Know what might break your Life Plan.

We know of several individuals who are quite wealthy but want to know that everything is going to be okay. So every year, they find it valuable to identify circumstances that might "break the plan." In this case, it could be helpful to add a large sum of imaginary spending *every* year to derail the plan. This can confirm the financial cushion they have.

Life doesn't always go as you expect, and bad things happen all the time. Consider what those might be now so you can be as prepared as possible for worst-case scenarios. Technically, an infinite number of challenges can occur, but some are much more likely than others.

For example, there is no mention in my financial plan of an attack by green Martians, but I do have considerations for death, disability, and job loss. I'm willing to roll the dice on the aliens. Seriously, though, it is a valuable exercise to decide which contingencies you want to factor into your plan.

Great confidence emerges from knowing what can derail the plan. This is intentionality in action.

Rule #5: Don't trick yourself with bad accounting.

Great accountants are not exactly known for being emotional, and there's a reason for that. Be careful of your inner *emotions accountant*. Let's call him Fred Feelings. Fred specializes in selective accounting, and he always shows you the number you want to see. The thing is, people often "hire" Fred Feelings because they are really excited about something, and he is known for helping them see only the numbers that support their case for making a major decision.

A common mistake people make when investing in real estate is doing a poor job of accounting for the gains or losses in their investment. I often hear people talk about the rental revenue they receive from their properties, but they deemphasize the cost of improvements and ongoing expenses.

If you have a rental property, be sure to do a thorough accounting of the income and expenses and compare that investment to other places you might invest those dollars. You may still conclude that real estate is the best place to invest, but you won't know unless you've done a thorough analysis of the cash flow. Fred Feelings just likes that real estate property because it's tangible, and the income flows in separate from the expenses.

Another requirement is accounting for the total cost of something you are buying.

I was once out for a boat ride with a good friend. His boat was a real beauty, and it wasn't cheap. We were cruising along, and he was telling me a story about hitting underwater floating debris, which caused damage to the boat.

I said, "Wow, that sounds like it was a really expensive repair."

His response was very sophisticated, and it wasn't consistent with what I often hear. "That repair was 'paid for' when I bought the boat."

Before he made that purchase, he did a thorough cost analysis including reasonable surprises that can come with use.

This illustrates the art of "not being surprised by things that aren't surprising" in action. Fred Feelings doesn't care about surprises later; he just wants to make you feel good now.

The opposite approach of Fred Feelings is Ruth Rational. Ruth is ruthless when it comes to being factual about accounting, and I like her approach. When accounting, be honest with yourself and use numbers that will give you true insight into your life and your decisions.

Rule #6: Don't overthink it.

I've given you a lot to think about in this chapter as it pertains to your decision-making. Be careful about overusing data and crippling your decision-making with paralysis by analysis. Because then you will likely abandon this approach.

Just make sure you have a trusted process or professional to help balance your emotions and the data to make the most informed decisions. When you pair your values, tendencies, and awareness of possible surprises with these concepts, you will start to see a strong plan developing.

Next, it's finally time for some investment tips. This is appropriate only now that I feel you are committed to intentionality, know your values, are clear about your tendencies, and are aware of some things that could otherwise trip you up. These are the characteristics of a person who is equipped to make decisions about their investments.

Life-Builders

This chapter gives some tips for creating a solid plan around your goals. Below are some questions to help you implement some of these ideas.

1. What is the "big thing" you want in the future that you can use to judge near-term opportunities against?

2. What values (such as status, safety, or adventure) do you typically seek when you choose to make a purchase sooner rather than later?

3. What is one thing you can do to better balance your emotions and your data when making financial decisions?

CHAPTER 8

THE INVESTMENT PART: ON-PURPOSE FINANCIAL MANAGEMENT

"Annual income twenty pounds, annual expenditure nineteen six, result happiness. Annual income twenty pounds, annual expenditure twenty pounds ought and six, result misery."

— *Charles Dickens*

F*inally*, we get to investment management, and it's exactly where it needs to be in the book. You've now been able to be thoughtful about who you are and the life you want to live. Now it's time to work on one of the tactics to drive that strategy forward: creating an On-Purpose financial plan aimed at driving your Life Plan to hit the specific goals you have created.

With that in mind, I have pulled together a list of my favorite guidelines for you to refer to as you make planning and investment decisions. This is far from a comprehensive investment strategy. Instead, it's meant to be useful guidance to help shape your decision-making around financial matters and investing.

It's my way of "un-intimidating" money management for you.

- **Carry your intentionality into your investment management.** My investment process does not seek to simply make the pile of money as big as possible. Don't get me wrong, we certainly want to earn our clients a lot of money. The important distinction is that we don't want to do all the planning outlined in this book and then have an investment management process that isn't consistent with our overall approach. In the preceding chapters, I outlined steps for creating intentional, values-driven plans, and your investment process should be no different.

- **Invest on purpose.** Just as we have an On-Purpose Method for planning, that mentality carries right through to your investments. Here are a few important things to think about in your investment plan.

- **Every single account must have a "job."** When you look at your financial statements and see every account you have, even a savings account or CD, you should be able to say specifically what each one is supposed to do and why. If this sounds overwhelming, it's not. One easy place to start with this is to name your accounts for the job they need to do. For example, do you remember my car-fire story from earlier? The money for our new cars came from an account that was literally labeled CARS on our statement. Lindsay and I have accounts named for travel, home improvement, kids' education, and even for our beach house that we don't own yet. You may not decide to get as granular on this as I do by dividing the accounts this specifically, but I hope you will apply this concept in some way.

Once you get close to retirement, if you really want tax efficiency, you should know which account you are drawing from in the different phases of retirement. During retirement, your tax situation can change significantly. This depends on when you take Social Security, how much you have in IRAs/401(k)s, pension income, and a number of other factors. There could be years where it would be advantageous to take from certain accounts based on your tax situation in that year. There can even be years in your retirement where it makes sense to make your withdrawals from a less tax-efficient account when your taxable income is expected to be lower. This can possibly include withdrawals from IRA/401(k) accounts and even Roth conversions, but this all depends on your individual tax situation and goals.

- **Treat your accounts like a farm.** Once you know the purpose of every account, carry that intentionality inside of the accounts to determine investment selection. You can do that by thinking of each account like it's a farm. A farmer knows which crops to leave alone because they are growing, and they know which ones are in a good position to harvest. By using this approach, you can apply the same rationale to your investment strategy.

  - **Grow:** Your growth allocation is likely to be mostly stocks, depending on your risk tolerance. These are your long-term investments. Younger people are likely to have more in the GROW bucket. As you can imagine, the assets earmarked for growth are more volatile and essentially not "ripe" enough to be harvested because you don't know how much they are going to be worth when you need them.

- **Harvest:** This approach is for the dollars earmarked to be taken out of the account and spent over the next several years. This highlights the importance of doing a cash-flow-based financial plan, so you know how much money you will need and when.

  You don't want to be in a position where you have to take money from your assets before they are ripe. Therefore, you must put considerable thought and effort into knowing how much money needs to come out of each account and when, and then invest those dollars in places that are traditionally less volatile. This increases the likelihood that those dollars will be there when you need them.

- **Fall in love with your emergency fund.** *Before* you determine how much goes into your other purpose-based accounts, you should establish a nice, juicy emergency fund.

  From an investment perspective, this account will likely be your least favorite right up until it is your most favorite, and then it will go back to being your least favorite account again. And that's by design. You will win by not losing.

  If you follow this somewhat unsexy approach, you will likely be rewarded for it at some point in your life. General guidance is to have an emergency fund sufficient to cover between three and six months of your total expenses.

  This is another great step in un-surprising your life. Job loss, major home repairs, health issues, and all kinds of other contingencies can pop up for people in a lifetime. An emergency fund that is financially strong will likely stay strong, whereas one that is financially average could be exposed and fall below average. A credit card or home equity loan is not a good substitute for an emergency fund. This will put you at the mercy of the lender, who can have higher interest rates, among other challenges.

When you have an emergency fund, specifically define the types of things it can be used for. It's amazing how we can become great salespeople to ourselves, and it would be best if you didn't schedule an "emergency" trip to the Caribbean with funds from this account after a long and difficult stretch at work.

- **Treat your extra cash like I treat potato chips.** I have no self-control with potato chips. Seriously. Especially Herr's Ripples. There is no such thing for me as just having one handful of chips. I've been known to eat a whole bag, more than once.

  My solution? We generally don't keep them in the house. Eliminate the threat, right?

  Apply the same solution to cash in your checking account. To avoid overdrafts, keep only enough to pay the month's bills in your checking account with a linked savings account. It's amazing how extra cash in savings can magically turn into an Amazon box on your front step.

  With this approach, you can be more intentional about your monthly spending.

- **Manage your debt.** My dad always had great guidance around debt.

  He said, "Debt is for things you can afford, and either you want to have them sooner than you have the cash or you are looking for a convenient way to pay for them. Debt is not for things you can't afford and want to have now."

  This might be an oversimplification or stating the obvious, but we can all get excited about big purchases. I totally get it.

  I don't have many rigid rules, but one I suggest you follow is to never carry credit-card debt with interest. If you grab a 0% interest offer, that's okay, but just remember they're not offering that promotion just to be nice. They're counting on the fact that you might not pay it off on time. If you view your credit card as simply an efficient means of payment that you always pay off monthly, you will put yourself in a strong position.

  There can be value in using low-interest debt in certain situations, as long as you are smart and careful borrowing that money.

- **Are you an investor or a gambler?** You can be both, but just be honest about it. Just as you narrowed down the overall allocation of the account between your Grow and Harvest dollars, you can further narrow down the Grow dollars. Sometimes, people want to gamble on a specific stock or a narrow sector of the economy such as biotechnology. These would be their possible "home run" positions. In our business, we call this speculation, and it's something I do with a portion of my own money. But you must carefully decide how much money should be available for speculation.

Being intentional about this means you are aware of the risks and know that these risks are limited to a specific corner of your growth allocation. Beware of getting overly excited about speculating with large amounts of money that will be important for you not to lose later. Over time, we've seen this happen with tech stocks, cryptocurrencies, and pot stocks.

- **Protect yourself from yourself.** The entire next chapter is dedicated to the concept of protecting yourself from yourself as it pertains to your daily financial decisions. This applies to your investments as well.

Portfolio manager Peter Lynch successfully ran Fidelity's Magellan Fund with a remarkable annual return of 29.2% from 1977 to 1990. This is my favorite of his quotes:

"Far more money has been lost by investors preparing for corrections or trying to anticipate corrections than has been lost in the corrections themselves."

When we work with clients, we make it clear that we plan to hold their investments through difficult market conditions. There may be some slight adjustments, but nothing huge that would try to time the market. If market-timing were easily repeatable, everybody would do it.

While 401(k) plans can be great in many ways, they have a major flaw. It can be difficult for investors to get access to good financial advice regarding these accounts, and this often leads to people making poor decisions. Be cautious about emotional investing in your 401(k), and use any resources available to help determine the right allocation for you. If in doubt, many 401(k)s offer target-date funds, which automatically adjust the investment allocation based on your time until retirement. These funds can be a little more expensive and are not without flaws, but in my opinion, they are better than having untrained individuals make important decisions on their 401(k) plans.

- **Avoid the "best day" approach.** Do you compare every day you live to the best day of your life? I hope not. Sounds like a ticket to misery to me.

"This dinner is so good…but it's not as good as the fresh seafood pasta dish from the award-winning restaurant where we dined in Italy."

Okay, maybe that's an exaggeration, but it applies to investing. Investors often compare their returns to the high watermark of their investments, the very highest account value they have seen. This can be a dangerous strategy. For one, you're almost never satisfied. Also, it can affect your behavior around portfolio decisions you make.

Instead of using the "best day" approach, your account should be invested for a specific purpose, and you should have an idea of whether that account is performing above or below a target rate of return that you've determined in advance. This is consistent with our philosophy of using good metrics and can help ease some of the discomfort you may have in looking at your investment statement.

- **Don't forget about tax efficiency.** Tax efficiency can apply to tax-deferred contributions to lower your taxable income, managing capital gains, tax-loss harvesting in taxable accounts, tax-efficient withdrawal strategies, and much more. When not managed effectively, taxes can steal significant wealth from you over time.

- **Don't invest solely based on your age.** A better approach is to use your goals and specific account purposes.

  Let's say someone in their late eighties has a moderate to aggressive risk tolerance and significantly more money than they could likely ever use during their lifetime. Assume that this person values generational wealth and leaving money to their heirs, who are in their forties.

  Given that this person is comfortable with this from a risk tolerance perspective, it could make sense to invest a portion of their money based on the age of their heirs instead. In this case, the heirs are in their forties and may have more time for the accounts to recover. It could be worth a family conversation, but as long as the customer understands the variability of returns, this is a strong example of using the account purpose to drive the investment allocation.

  Liquidation strategy could also play a role in how funds are allocated. Many people think that their retirement accounts will be eligible for withdrawals immediately after retirement, but as I mentioned earlier, there may be more tax-efficient considerations. It could be worth waiting until the person hits their required minimum distribution age, which is either age 73 or 75, depending on their birth year.

- **You can only invest each dollar in one place.** Sometimes, clients have hard decisions to make about certain investments. It could be company stock, an investment with sentimental value, or a stock you've held for a long time.

  Ask yourself this question: "Is this the very best place I can invest these dollars?"

  While you may enjoy working for your company, position concentrations in company stock aren't always the wisest investment. Also, you may want to ask yourself whether the potential cost of sentimentality is worth holding an investment with a personal connection.

In summary, always remember *why* you are investing. Investing is not something that exists on its own but one of many tactics you can use to help drive your great Life Plan forward.

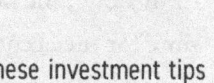

Life-Builders

1. What is your plan for implementing these investment tips within your Life Plan?

2. Are your accounts properly aimed to fund the goals that are most important to you? If not, pick one important goal you would like to fund, and select investments (on your own or with the help of an advisor) that are appropriate from a risk perspective to fund it.

STEP 3

Protect Yourself

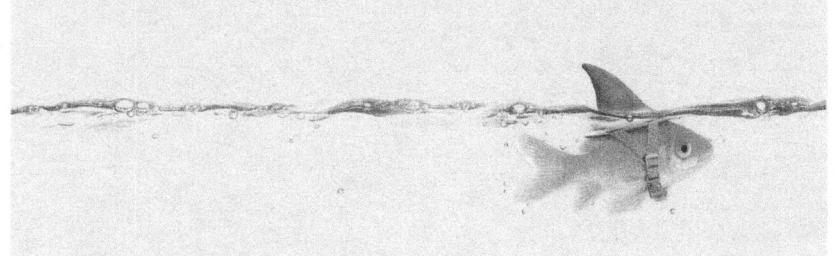

CHAPTER 9

MANAGE YOUR BEHAVIOR AFTER THE PLAN

*"If you do not tell the truth about yourself, you cannot tell
it about other people."*

— *Virginia Woolf*

When you've finished this book and resume real life, you
will have many choices to make. This chapter is designed
to help *protect you from yourself* and to inspire you to make bold,
intentional choices to live an amazing life.

How Your History Impacts Your Habits

A person's life experiences significantly affect their decision-making around planning, spending, and saving. It's interesting to
see how people react to their parents' spending habits. In some
cases, our clients want to model them; in other cases, they prefer
to go completely in the opposite direction. And some people
feel guilty for spending differently than their parents did.

This is certainly something to consider. Your parents lived in
a different time and may have had very different lives. If you
feel guilty for choosing a different path than your parents did,

take some time to explore why you feel that way. It's better to discover this pattern now than to subconsciously try to live your parents' values when they may not align with your goals and ambitions.

There are other ways to honor your parents. Financially speaking, what can you hold on to that your parents did well? What should you let go of? Live your own life and keep an eye on this pattern if this applies to you.

Another area that plays a significant role in personal spending is our experience with hardship. Understandably, some people's perception of the fragility of life has been affected by a significant challenge they have endured. For example, many of our clients who are cancer survivors tend to have a "front-load the fun" mentality.

Like with anything, you should be aware of where this is useful and where it may be overdone. When done with intentionality and moderation, you can use your hardship to build a better future. Ask yourself the following three questions now to build a strategy for moving forward.

- How does this serve me?
- How does this challenge me?
- What can I apply from my life experience moving forward?

Don't lose awareness of the role your personal history plays in your Life Planning and daily decision-making.

Knowing Your Patterns

We all have behavior patterns that we should start to pay more attention to.

- When Alicia has had a crappy day at work and the kids are fighting all evening, she turns to a little online retail therapy to make her feel better.

- Geoff and Sandy's go-to dinner on busy activity nights for the kids is takeout from the local burger joint.

- Bart loves the idea of eating healthily and cheaply, but because he works late and likes to sleep in, he just doesn't feel like packing his lunch in the morning. Lunches out five days per week are not uncommon.

- Jake and Leslie like drinking good wine. They generally try not to drink alcohol on weeknights, but after managing work stress and kids' activities, the wine can start to flow at the end of each day.

Un-surprising your spending patterns can feel amazing. Just by starting with simple awareness, you may find benefits. When these patterns start to set in, they can serve as a sign that it's time to make a change elsewhere in your life. These types of patterns can get expensive in terms of money, health, and relationships. They are worth observing.

- What are five spending patterns you have that may be costing more than just money?

- How will you notice them when you are "in the heat of the moment"?

- What rule can you create to address each of these patterns to help get the outcomes you hope for?

Balance & Trade-Offs

It's worth mentioning again that good financial management is simply a big game of trade-offs. You are continuously faced with life and money decisions. Train yourself to think about the trade-offs you are making in terms of future opportunities and experiences.

However, remember that your analysis in the moment is not always rational. Keep an eye out for a tricky common behavior trap that can derail an otherwise intentional plan. It's time to introduce the concept I call "furgency."

What Is Furgency?

Take the word *urgency*, as in how you feel about that big thing you really "need," then add the word *false* in front of it: false + urgency. Squeeze them together, and you get *furgency*.

Furgency is where your emotions hijack your brain and make you feel like a move you are about to make is part of your intentional plan when it may not be.

You are an excellent salesperson for yourself. Some seemingly amazing opportunity comes your way, and everything in the universe starts telling you that you need it. And the justification starts coming in…hard. You start making the case that this is a perfect fit, and the emotions around it are strong.

Sometimes a client calls in with something completely outside of their original plan and many reasons why it needs to happen…and it needs to happen *right now*. And in some cases, it IS the right thing.

Your life won't go exactly to plan, and there will be some times you should deviate. Just be aware of when you might be tricking yourself in the name of something that doesn't align with what you truly want or takes money away from future spending that will benefit you more.

To help you be careful around this tendency, I'm going to share six rules for a Furgency Check.

1. **Follow the 24-hour rule.** Time will tell you if it's actually urgent. Your furgency is allowing for made-up deadlines and pushy sales pitches to seem more credible. Give it time. And if it can wait 24 hours, isn't that the definition of "not urgent" for a lot of things?

2. **Bounce it off an uninterested party.** Just do this to say you did. After all, you probably won't listen to them anyway because your furgency is so strong. Bring it to the friend who says what everybody else is thinking. Maybe they will actually tell you something valuable.

3. **Take a look at your history.** Recall examples of other items you later realized were furgent. Does this purchase seem like those? Again, just be intentional about it when you can. You don't have to be super rigid; just keep an eye on it.

4. **Remember what it took to get those dollars you would be spending.** After all, you're not really spending money; in some ways, you're spending time. How long did you have to work to make enough money to buy this thing? Or how long did the person who gave you that money

have to work for it? Also consider taxes that would have to be paid.

5. **Think about trade-offs.** Your furgent thing comes at a future cost. What will you be giving up in terms of future items, experiences, or feelings of security in exchange for this thing?

6. **Use the BAC Rule.** You might assume the BAC stands for something financial like budget, accumulate, and compound. Wrong. It's the BAC you probably know: blood alcohol content. Be careful shopping when you are a little tipsy! Lindsay and I call it the Amazon Cocktail Cart, and it's real. Alcohol is a powerful furgency generator, so be aware of that. (You can always return it, I guess.)

How to Make Good "Bad" Financial Decisions

Let's say you decide there is something that might be furgent or even totally out there, but you really want to do it anyway. Be a mindful Maxer then!

There will be times when you want to make an impulsive decision that's right for you. And that's okay, if you follow this guidance:

- It's okay if you make a decision that is good for you but would be bad for others if they made the same decision. Own it! That's what can make life fun.

- Make it measurable. Know your numbers so you can make an educated decision.

- Consciously accept the trade-off as a future version of yourself. Consider your viewpoint of this decision years from now and argue both sides of it.

- Invite some trusted outsiders to challenge it. Either they will talk you out of it, or you'll decide it's still a good idea.

When Something Bad Happens, Be Prepared for Something Bad to Happen

This is just another piece of the un-surprising process. Bad things tend to happen in clumps (car breaks down, job loss), so it's important to be mentally prepared for that. In your financial life, this highlights the value of an emergency fund as well as contingency planning.

If you've worked through a variety of contingencies in your plan, and you have money set aside to cover them even if a few happen at once, I have a feeling you will see an uptick in your confidence related to clarity around the future.

MATM

MATM stands for the "move after the move." Remember that the next financial decision you make is likely not the last one you will ever make. There will be a next move. Keeping this in mind can help remove any pressure around making the perfect decision. Sure, we all want to make great decisions on the first try, but an abundant and confident approach will give you more faith and hope that things will unfold positively for you…even if it happens in a different way than you planned.

Self-Gratitude Journaling

Journaling has changed my life. As I mentioned earlier, I've always been one for doing hard things such as competing in triathlons; managing a business; and being a dedicated, thoughtful husband and dad. What I didn't mention is that I was not giving myself any credit for it. This was a problem, but since then I've made a subtle but important change. Celebrating my own efforts has given me a more abundant mindset.

Just as you would show appreciation for someone you care about, there is value in showing appreciation for the effort you have given for your own goals.

Gratitude also serves as amazing fuel. I suggest you start keeping a journal of the hard or even mundane things you do to support the life you desire. You can start by celebrating all the choices you will make from what you learn in this book.

Here are some examples of my self-gratitude journal entries:

- "Glad I pushed myself to go on that run this morning when I didn't want to. I feel great now."
- "So grateful for our family vacation in Colorado. The splurges were worth it. I'm so glad we worked so hard to be able to do this."
- "Lots of good self-care and rest this weekend. I needed it!"
- "I cut down on my mindless scrolling this week."

It's healthy to remind yourself of the sacrifices and tough choices you make in the name of something that's important to you.

Mind Traps (Cognitive Biases)

Behavioral finance covers many common cognitive biases, which are defined as systematic errors in thinking when people process and interpret information in the world around them.

Instead of using the term "cognitive bias" (you know by now that I don't like to use big words when small words get us to the same or better place), I like to refer to these things as **mind traps**.

Here are a few mind traps to be aware of.

- **Anchoring Bias:** This mind trap happens when we rely too heavily on the first piece of information we receive when making a decision. Let's say you saw a shirt at the store that was originally priced at $80, but now it's $55. You might see this as a great deal due to the initial higher price even if the item is not worth $80.

- **Confirmation Bias:** This is the tendency to have preexisting beliefs and then take only the information that supports those beliefs. We often see this with political opinions. In my work, we see confirmation bias a lot as we seek to protect people from their own politics. Too often, when the stock market goes down, a person may say, "See, that's because [whoever is in office at the time] is president!" Confirmation bias can lead to poor investment decision-making.

- **Endowment Effect:** This is where you might value something more highly just because you already own it, and you ignore its objective market value. This can cause people to hold on to property or other assets, including stocks, longer than might be advisable. In the example of a car or a house, people sometimes resist selling it at market

125

value because their personal attachment causes them to overvalue it.

- **Overconfidence Bias:** This bias leads us to overestimate our knowledge, ability, or the accuracy of our predictions. For example, you might overestimate your ability to pick winning stocks based on a few past successes, leading to riskier financial decisions than are warranted by your actual expertise.

- **Status Quo Bias:** This refers to the preference for keeping things the way they are and avoiding change. For example, many people stick with the same bank, credit card, or financial advisor because it feels more comfortable than exploring something new.

Abundance

While you will use the scarcity of time as part of your planning, you should balance that with abundance and appreciation.

A scarcity mindset can leave you chasing things and often spending money to fill perceived gaps in your life. Be sure to spend time feeling gratitude and appreciation for everything you have.

Remember that carrying intentionality through your daily living will be a key to long-term success in creating your fulfilling life. It won't always be perfect, but remember, there is always a move after the move.

Life-Builders

While most of us focus on protecting ourselves from external threats, many of the things that can keep us from reaching our goals come from within. Answer the questions below to give yourself more clarity around ways you can protect yourself from behaviors that could derail you.

1. List three spending patterns you recognize in yourself.

2. List three spending patterns you recognize in your partner (or a very important person in your life).

3. How can you adjust or be aware of these spending patterns to make sound financial decisions?

4. What is a good "bad" financial decision you have made recently?

CHAPTER 10

BRING IT ALL TOGETHER

"I have been impressed with the urgency of doing.
Knowing is not enough; we must apply.
Being willing is not enough; we must do."

— *Leonardo da Vinci*

A s this book comes to a close, my biggest wish for you is that you have a broadened perspective of what it will take to create a wonderful life and how to be intentional in your planning so you stay on track and on purpose.

Let's be clear: This is not a recipe for a perfect life, and no doubt there will be some things at the end that you will do differently. However, let's do one last round of un-surprising by reviewing the most common end-of-life regrets so you can learn something from them.

Living a Life Without Regrets

In his book *Resisting Happiness*, Matthew Kelly asked a group of hospice nurses what people who are dying say they wish they had done differently in their lives. Here are some of the top wishes:

- I wish I'd had the courage to just be myself.

- I wish I had taken better care of myself.

- I wish I had spent more time with the people I love.

- I wish I hadn't spent so much time working.

- I wish I hadn't spent so much time worrying about things that never happened.

- I wish I had cared less about what other people thought.

- I wish I had quit my job and found something I really enjoyed doing.

- I wish I had touched more lives.

- I wish I had traveled more.

- I wish I had lived more in the moment.

By working backward to avoid end-of-life regrets like these, you can start now with a well-crafted intention on planning your life and making financial choices that reflect your most important values.

Going from on Track to on Purpose

It's time to turn the concepts you've learned in this book into action.

We began with the question "Am I on track?"

By now, I hope you have some ideas for feeling more on track. But more importantly, I hope you now know what it takes to live on purpose. An intentional, values-driven life awaits you with a clear, data-driven path that allows you to check in with your emotions before making important financial decisions.

When you do, you'll free up your time to make room for more wonderful moments—and I'll bet some good surprises, too.

Five Commitments

Before you put this book down, take a moment to fill in the blanks below. Making the following five commitments about how you will live your life intentionally will spark action.

1. I commit to spending more time with _____.

2. I will improve _____ in my health by doing _____.

3. The first financial surprise I'm going to stop being surprised by and plan for is _____.

4. I will do the values exercise by ____/____ [date].

5. I will talk to my partner about something I learned in this book by ____/____ [date].

When the Work Is Done

It's about time to wrap this up, so I'm going to tell you a quick story that helps illustrate where I want you to land.

It was 2004, and my wife Lindsay was an event planner for the Leukemia & Lymphoma Society. I remember one autumn Saturday night, we were at a black-tie fundraiser Lindsay had planned at a beautiful Center City Philadelphia hotel. We were in this big, elegant ballroom having a great time; it was a truly incredible event. We were dancing, and I was chowing down on the butlered hors d'oeuvres, like I normally do.

(By the way, here's a pro tip for when you are at an event like this or a wedding: Stand right by the door that the hors d'oeuvres are coming out of. You will have a front-row seat to all the best hot snacks you can eat!)

About halfway through the night, I turned to Lindsay and said, "This event is absolutely amazing, but I have one question. This is your event, so why are you not working?"

I'm so smooth, right?

But her response rolled easily and proudly off her tongue. "If I didn't do my job, there would be work to do."

The event had been properly planned, and it was now ours to enjoy.

That, my friend, is my wish for you. And it's possible.

Our clients are often shocked about how smooth their final retirement meeting is. We review the plan and their income stream. We may also discuss important mental health considerations in the transition to retired life. But the work has been done.

And with some intentionality and balance—and un-surprising some surprises—a fulfilling and smooth retirement is possible for you, too. After all, when you've chosen to embrace your planning from the lens of a Life Plan, you can rest assured you are on the right track for living a fulfilling life aligned with your most important values and dreams.

REFERENCES

1,000 Hours Outside. "75% of the Time We Spend with Our Kids in Our Lifetime Will Be Spent by Age 12." Blog. 1000HoursOutside.com. Accessed August 30, 2024. https://www.1000hoursoutside.com/blog/time-with-kids-before-age-12.

Armenta, Christina, Katherine Jacobs Bao, Sonja Lyubomirsky, and Kennon M. Sheldon. 2014. "Is Lasting Change Possible? Lessons from the Hedonic Adaptation Prevention Model." In *Stability of Happiness*, 57–74. Academic Press.

Belludi, Nagesh. 2016. "The Drunkard's Search or the Streetlight Effect [Cognitive Bias]." Right Attitudes, February 26, 2016. https://www.rightattitudes.com/2016/02/26/drunkard-search-streetlight-effect/.

Covey, Stephen. 1989. *The Seven Habits of Highly Effective People*. Simon & Schuster.

Fisher, Jen. 2015. "Workplace Burnout Survey: Burnout Without Borders." Deloitte. https://www2.deloitte.com/us/en/pages/about-deloitte/articles/burnout-survey.html.

Goldstein, Michael. 2019. "The Triumph of the Roller Bag." *Forbes*, April 15, 2019. https://www.forbes.com/sites/michaelgoldstein/2019/04/15/the-triumph-of-the-roller-bag/.

Harris, Dan. 2014. *10% Happier*. It Books.

International Friendships. "Two Sides of Time: Task-Oriented Cultures vs. Event-Oriented Cultures." May 24, 2022. https://www.ifipartners.org/cross-cultural/two-sides-of-time.

Joel, Billy. "We Didn't Start the Fire." *Storm Front*. Produced by Mick Jones. Columbia. Released as a single on September 18, 1989.

Jones, Heather. 2024. "Managing Dyslexia and ADHD." VeryWellHealth, February 23, 2024. https://www.verywellhealth.com/adhd-and-dyslexia-5207990.

Junius. 1929. "Office Cat." *Cambridge City Tribune*, January 17, 1929.

Kelly, Matthew. 2016. *Resisting Happiness.* Blue Sparrow Books.

Lasseter, John, dir. 2006. *Cars.* Buena Vista Pictures Distribution.

Li, Yun. 2023. "Investing Legend Peter Lynch on the Investments He Regrets Not Making in Recent Years." CNBC, April 25, 2023. https://www.cnbc.com/2023/04/25/investing-legend-peter-lynch-on-the-investments-he-regrets-not-making-in-recent-years.html.

Piaget, Jean. 1954. *The Construction of Reality in the Child.* Translated by Margaret Cook. Basic Books.

Rogers, Katie. 2016. "Boaty McBoatface: What You Get When You Let the Internet Decide." *New York Times*, March 21, 2016. https://www.nytimes.com/2016/03/22/world/europe/boaty-mcboatface-what-you-get-when-you-let-the-internet-decide.html.

Sharkey, Joe. 2010. "Reinventing the Suitcase by Adding the Wheel," *New York Times.* October 2, 2010. https://www.nytimes.com/2010/10/05/business/05road.html.

Tversky, Amos, and Daniel Kahneman. 1974. "Judgment under Uncertainty: Heuristics and Biases: Biases in Judgments Reveal Some Heuristics of Thinking under Uncertainty." *Science*, 185 (4157): 1124–1131.

Urban, Tim. 2015. "The Tail End." *Wait But Why*, December 11, 2015. https://waitbutwhy.com/2015/12/the-tail-end.html.

Williams, Geoff. 2023. "The Best Time to Buy Everything." *U.S. News*, November 9, 2023. https://money.usnews.com/money/personal-finance/saving-and-budgeting/articles/the-best-time-of-year-to-buy-everything.

ABOUT THE AUTHOR

 JAY WHEELER is president of Wheeler Financial and serves as their senior financial advisor. He has a bachelor's degree from the University of Delaware and holds the Accredited Investment Fiduciary (AIF) certification. Additionally, he completed the Behavioral Financial Advice program through think2perform and the certificate program in Behavioral Economics: Consumer Choice and Decision Making through Wharton Executive Education.

Jay writes extensively for the "Wheeler Weekly Newsletter" and "Money Monday Blog" and has published articles in *Forbes* and other publications.

Jay's passion resides in the "human side" of financial management, and he is driven by making personal connections with his clients and understanding their pain points as well as their dreams.

He sits on the board of the Wilmington Tax Group and several charitable organizations.

Outside of work, he values being a dedicated husband and dad. His interests include trail running, hiking, gardening, music, and time spent laughing with family and friends.

ACKNOWLEDGMENTS

TO MY AMAZING wife Lindsay and our wonderful children, Grady and Anna: I had no idea I could love so much. Thank you for being uniquely you. Your support of this book and everything I do is truly appreciated.

I am also fortunate beyond measure to have such outstanding parents, brothers, extended family, and friends.

To our Wheeler Financial Team: You take your roles at Wheeler Financial personally, and that transcends any business metrics. I am so grateful to be surrounded by such great human beings every day. Without your contribution, this book would have stayed locked in my laptop forever.

To our Wheeler Financial clients: It's truly rewarding to be a part of your lives. You are the best. I have learned and grown so much from our partnerships, and this book is a reflection of these wonderful relationships.

To Catherine Gregory, Nathan Joblin, and the team at Modern Wisdom Press: Your fabulous and organized book coaching process was outdone only by your compassion and the personal connection you created with me as an author.

Thank you.

THANK YOU

Dear Reader,

Thank you for reading my book. I built the framework in this book to spark a new way of thinking about your life and financial planning. I hope you are inspired with some new ideas about how to align your planning to your life vision and values. And now, you'll need to do some work to implement the tools and stay accountable.

Wheeler Financial partners with our clients to help guide them through both the technical and human details of financial planning and management. We work best with delegators who value having a professional partner to ensure that the details of their Life Plan are handled with care and accuracy.

To learn more about becoming a Wheeler Financial client, contact us through our website at www.WheelerFinancial-llc.com/contact.

If you would enjoy reading more content from me, check out my "Wheeler Weekly" newsletter. To sign up for these informative weekly emails at no charge, go to:

www.WheelerFinancial-llc/wheeler_weekly

And finally, as a special gift for reading my book, I want to help you adopt some savvy saving tips while spending. After all, you can't invest a dollar you've already spent, so spending wisely is one of my favorite hacks for saving you in the long run! Go to this link for the free download: www.WheelerFinancial-llc.com/thank_you_gift.

ABOUT
MODERN WISDOM PRESS

FOUNDED BY Catherine Gregory and Nathan Joblin in 2019, Modern Wisdom Press is dedicated to elevating conscious voices by empowering visionary leaders and subject matter experts to find clarity, ease, and joy in writing and publishing their transformational nonfiction books.

Our values and core principles are rooted in conscious leadership, which begins with self-awareness and intentionality, awakening more fulfillment and purpose in your life and those you lead. We support aspiring authors who are here to make a positive impact, with the ripple effect benefiting not only their readers but also their families, communities, and beyond.

modern wisdom
PRESS